Break time

devotions for young women

written by: amanda cowles
illustrations by: amylee weeks

CHRISTIAN ART PUBLISHERS

Break Time

Published by Christian Art Publishers
PO Box 1599, Vereeniging, 1930, RSA

Text © 2015 Amanda Cowles
Art © 2015 Amylee Weeks
All rights reserved.

Scripture quotations are taken from the *Holy Bible*, New International
Version® NIV®. Copyright © 1973, 1978, 1984, 2011 by International
Bible Society. Used by permission of Biblica, Inc.® All rights reserved
worldwide.

Printed in China

ISBN 978-1-4321-1430-5

17 18 19 20 21 22 23 24 25 26 – 10 9 8 7 6 5 4 3 2 1

for my mom.
love, a.c.

Your love, O LORD,
reaches to the
heavens, Your
faithfulness
to the skies.

Psalm 36:5

january

BE STILL

Take this moment to be still and to simply acknowledge the Great I Am. Breathe deep. Acknowledge Him as Creator, as Holder of this single moment in time. He is the One who sustains, the One who brings peace. God.

You were not meant to spend even a single moment outside of the presence of God. Your heart becomes restless, anxious, and uneasy when you forget Him. But when you stop, when you listen for the sound of His heart, yours melts. In the stillness, and to your great awe, you find He is as gentle as He is mighty and as forgiving as He is just.

Now rest in the quiet stillness that comes from the presence of the One who loves you most.

. . .

"Be still, and know that I am God."
Psalm 46:10

BE YOU

Christ came that you may have life and that you may have it to the full. So be you!

Be the you God had in mind when He said, "This. Her. She is the one I want in My life. Heaven needs her. Her brothers and sisters need her."

You fill a need. You fill a place in the heart of God that only you can fill. But when you pull into your shell, when you hide from the world, creation becomes less than intended. So remember you belong.

You are uniquely you on purpose and FOR a purpose. God's purpose. And His definition of you is the ONLY definition that matters, because it's the only definition that's true.

. . .

In fact God has arranged the parts in the body, every one of them, just as He wanted them to be. If they were all one part, where would the body be? As it is, there are many parts, but one body.

1 Corinthians 12:18-20

january 3

GOD WANTS YOU TO BLOOM

Consider the lilies. Consider the Son.
Consider an unhindered relationship. A
simple experience with no expectations.
No need to prove worth or purpose. No
need to make up for lost time. The
lilies. They simply are. They are a lovely example of a life dependent on God,
of a life unhindered by expectations or
the curious eyes of onlookers.

They do not struggle to know or to understand the God who feeds their roots
or shines the sun. They simply accept
His presence and experience His touch
on their lives. Their very existence is
a praise and a testament to His.

May you consider the lilies and experience simply the unhindered presence
of God.

. . .

"See how the lilies
of the field grow ... "
Matthew 6:28

BLESSED ASSURANCE

Faith in God leads to faithfulness in every area of your life. In faith you acknowledge the truth about God and live life accordingly. Your confidence lies in the unfailing reality of God's existence, in His promises, and in His never-giving-up faithfulness to His creations.

Faith does the right thing because it's the right thing without regard to self or circumstance. Its answer to God is always yes.

A steady walk in faith develops stability of feelings and actions. You cease to be the double-minded self of your past and become, instead, an anchor in an otherwise unsteady world.

To the skeptic faith can only smile, because proof is etched on the heart. Faith knows the promises of God are true.

. . .

Now faith is being sure of what we hope for and certain of what we do not see.

Hebrews 11:1

WHEN YOU PRAY

Prayer and thankfulness. These are the actions of your life that say, "Yes, Lord. You are in control. Always. You are present and You are more than enough."

Prayer and thankfulness are the fruit of trust in a God who is more than you can hope to wrap your mind around. You pray and you are thankful, because though you do not fully understand, you fully trust that you are fully loved. And His love doesn't need to be understood, only accepted and – prayerfully, continually, gratefully – experienced.

You acknowledge His presence and acknowledge His ways as better than your own, His eye on your life as sufficient. No need to fret over your naiveté, the presence of God means all is well.

. . .

Pray continually, give thanks in all circumstances; for this is God's will for you in Christ Jesus.

1 Thessalonians 5:17-18

YOU ARE LOVED

Your forever faithful God, His presence is solid, persistent. His love toward you never weakens and is perfect in every way.

He will never lose interest or care an ounce less for your well-being than He does right now. God loves you more than any other is capable of loving you, and He sees you in every moment of every day.

You mustn't underestimate God's ability to love. You mustn't underestimate the immediacy of His presence or the depth of fellowship offered you.

Rather, take time to sit with Him. To listen. To meditate on the greatness that is God and allow yourself to be overwhelmed, not by life's uncertainties, not by worries of the day, but by the nearness of God – Faithful Redeemer.

. . .

Your love, LORD, reaches to the heavens,
Your faithfulness to the skies.

Psalm 36:5

A GREAT HOPE

Today the world is broken. Man set himself in the place of God and the human race ran amok. Disaster overwhelms and you shake your fist at God. You want to know, "Why have You allowed this evil? Why have You allowed this pain?"

Humanity has been unfaithful and often accuses God of negligence; but He is forever faithful and in His great compassion you find your hope.

You find hope in the light of Christ — in the light of the cross. In the light of a God willing to suffer your consequences. In your deepest of deeps you know, great is His unfailing love!

His plan is perfect. Even now He is making all things right.

. . .

Because of the LORD's great
love we are not consumed, for
His compassions never fail.

Lamentations 3:22

A PLACE IN HIS STORY

It is no accident that you long for purpose in your life. You were created for purpose. You were created as part of God's story.

He uses purpose to build individual relationships with His children, and He uses purpose to build the collective nature of His church.

Don't believe for a moment that your role is insignificant. Every one is significant. Every life matters.

Pray for understanding and discernment. Pray for and about the desires of your heart, trusting they are placed there by the God who knows more about you and your eternity than you can begin to comprehend.

More than anything, trust the Creator. Trust His omniscience. The story is His and one day you will see its perfection.

. . .

We are God's workmanship, created in Christ Jesus to do good works, which God prepared in advance for us to do.

Ephesians 2:10

WHEN YOU FIND HIM

In quiet moments you steal away and you wait for God. You listen. You wonder. And in an instant you are swept away by the truth that God is not in your mind. He is not made up. He is not the creation, but the Creator.

Overwhelmed, you are no longer satisfied to meet with God as you have met Him before. You are no longer satisfied with the version of Him you have imagined and long, rather, for the great I Am Himself. You do not want a counterfeit.

He offers you this rare glimpse into eternity and your heart hungers for more. This is the Lord you seek. You want to listen and hear His voice with the deepest places of your soul.

. . .

"You will seek Me and find Me when you seek Me with all your heart."

Jeremiah 29:13

ONLY HE CAN SATISFY

You were created with a deep need in your life for the presence of God. Without Him, you live in response to an emptiness, a hunger, that He alone can fill.

As long as you are driven by the emptiness, your actions are to and from yourself; you act in response to a sense of self-preservation.

But when you begin to understand yourself with God as your center, He fills you and you respond to life out of the overflow of His presence rather than an emptiness within. Your thoughts turn out, not in, and you become a contributor to life rather than needing to be contributed to. In the contribution, in the overflow, you find purpose. This is the place where contentment abounds.

. . .

He satisfies the thirsty and fills
the hungry with good things.

Psalm 107:9

POUR OUT YOUR HEART

Pour out your heart to God. Pour out to Him your joys, your fears, your thoughts of every kind. Pour out to Him praise, adoration of His name.

The praises you sing, your heart cries, may feel inadequate. But what makes communion perfect to God's heart is the heart from which it flows, the motivation from which it is born.

And when you pour out to God, He pours out to you. He makes your worship a perfect offering. He purifies. He restores. He never, ever rejects a heart that is seeking His own.

So do not hold back in your relationship with Him. Do not fear where you should go or what you should say. He will lead the way.

. . .

Continue to work out your salvation
with fear and trembling, for it is
God who works in you to will and
to act according to His good purpose.

Philippians 2:12-13

MAKE EVERY EFFORT

God created such a variety of personalities and backstories that unity among all believers comes as quite the feat. And yet the church is encouraged by Paul to "keep the unity of the Spirit through the bond of peace."

The more fully you come to know God, the more necessary unity becomes. It simply does not work for believers to live in discord. The more you know and understand the common bond shared in Christ, the more inappropriate disunity must seem. Disunity should deeply grieve sincere believers. What connects is not merely a common idea, but the Spirit of God.

There will be disagreements to resolve. There will be misunderstandings to set right. But in the end there must never be disunity.

Make every effort.

. . .

Make every effort to keep the unity of the Spirit through the bond of peace.
Ephesians 4:3

HE IS WATCHING OVER YOU

The morning dawns and you sit in expectation. You wonder what God will say. You wait. You watch. Your spiritual eyes are opened. Lean in to the experience. Expect to see God. Expect for Him to come. Let nothing stand in the way of your waiting and watching daily for God.

The earth waits for His return and your soul waits to experience Him today. Every day. Anything less than God is simply not worth the exchange. What has been created can never fill the places of your soul meant for the Creator. No substitutes.

God is pleased that you wait for Him. That you anticipate His purpose. His return. He is pleased when you place your faith in His presence, His promise, His plan.

. . .

My soul waits for the Lord more than watchmen wait for the morning, more than watchmen wait for the morning.

Psalm 130:6

SHOW RESPECT

To grant respect when respect has not been earned stings a wounded pride. You want to retaliate or hide away when insulted or belittled or overlooked. How often have you said, "I will show them respect when they've shown it to me"?

And then the moment of truth. Surely you are meant to respect others because of your respect for God. Surely God's commitment and love to them should be more important than personal feelings.

Show respect to the ones God loves. Period. And God so loved the world.

Be a safe place. A person who protects reputations, who lifts others up and does not tear them down.

Be a person who respects people, because you are a person who respects God.

. . .

Be kind and compassionate to one
another, forgiving each other,
just as in Christ God forgave you.

Ephesians 4:32

OFFER YOUR BEST

Make a decided effort to offer the best of yourself throughout this day. This is an act of respect and reverence for God. An act of worship. And regardless of circumstance, regardless of feelings, regardless of how great or small the act may seem, offer God your best and accept the grace He gives, which enables you to follow through.

You are equipped for the work God prepared for you. Every unforeseen situation is foreseen by God. And what seems insignificant to you may mean a great deal to the plan God has for your life, or the plan God has for the life of another.

Offer your best. Trust His grace. This is your act of worship.

. . .

Never be lacking in zeal, but keep your spiritual fervor, serving the Lord.

Romans 12:11

A CHANGED HEART

Others observe the truth about God in the sincere heart change of believers. A heart changed by God isn't hard. Rather, it is full of compassion, patience, and mercy.

A changed heart is inviting. It treats all people with kind respect. Its own confidence and acceptance lies in an intimate relationship with God.

The heart turned toward God isn't looking for the approval of others, yet it heaps approval and love to those who sit in need of grace, its life an overflow of daily worship to God.

You are accepted. You are loved. You are wanted. These are the words every heart waits to hear. These are the words Christ whispers to your soul.

. . .

Create in me a pure heart, O God,
and renew a steadfast spirit within me.

Psalm 51:10

BLESSINGS FROM GOD

It is God's will that you have access to Him. He offered Himself to Adam, to Abraham, to David. Christ came that you may know God more fully. By the Spirit He remains Emmanuel, God with us.

And in this constant presence of God, remember to pray for His blessing. Ask Him to shine His face on those you love.

When you say yes to God, you say yes to a direct relationship with the Creator. You gain access.

You are in God's presence and you may ask for His blessings in your life. You may ask for God to turn His face to your children, your parents, your friends. It is your privilege to go to Him and His pleasure to respond.

. . .

The LORD bless you and keep you; the LORD make His face shine upon you and be gracious to you; the LORD turn His face toward you and give you peace."

Numbers 6:24-26

SING A NEW SONG!

In each believer there is a new song waiting to be sung. A song that sings in sweet communion from your heart to God's. A song of life redeemed and life renewed.

These life songs move you from one moment to the next. You are walking out your salvation, learning what life with Christ means. And your life, your songs of praise and appreciation, are made new and fresh as you go. Each new understanding brings a new verse to the life you live. Every life lesson enhances your song.

Together our songs sing a sweet chorus to our King. His plan is perfect, His vision infinite. So continue to work out your salvation. Know that God is for you. And sing!

. . .

Sing to the LORD a new song.
Psalm 98:1

TRUST IN THE LORD

You trust God and you lean on His ability to know all things. Still, you find some instances of trust easier than others.

It's easier to trust, for instance, when you secretly believe you can predict the outcome or retain a certain amount of control. But in truth, this isn't trust at all. It merely nurtures a weak and quite dishonest faith. Untried trust produces a Christian with little experience to back her beliefs.

But if you want your relationship with God to progress and be real to you, you must allow room to experience His hand in your life. God refines your faith into what He has always meant it to be.

There is freedom when you allow God to be God.

. . .

Trust in the Lord with all your heart
and lean not on your own understanding.

Proverbs 3:5

GOD UPHOLDS YOU

Whatever God has called you to, He does not leave you to do it alone. He promises to uphold you. His great desire is always to make Himself known.

So do not lose sight of the God who has chosen you. Do not be overwhelmed when the world seems too much and when you fear you are simply not enough.

God is more than enough and He has not set the world into motion only to turn His face from it now.

He has not lost sight of you and you must not lose sight of Him. Set your faith to the One who is love incarnate. Remember, His story is the beginning and the end and He holds every moment in-between.

. . .

"So do not fear, for I am with you; do not be dismayed, for I am your God. I will strengthen you and help you; I will uphold you with My righteous right hand."

Isaiah 41:10

PRAISE THE LORD!

What an honor that you are invited to praise the Lord! What an honor that you are invited into the presence of the One who made it all.

Lift up your hands! It was God who thought of you first. He is the One who first saw your form, saw you, and called your creation good.

The quiet moments given to God and the jubilant moments of praise, these are the times that make your bond with Him real.

Precious moments between your heart and His. No one can take this from you.

To know God is personal, and you are invited to know Him. You are invited to praise Him. You are invited to experience His touch on your life every day.

. . .

Lift up your hands in the
sanctuary and praise the LORD.

Psalm 134:2

HE HUMBLES YOU

In God's great mercy He takes you to a low place, a place where your heart may be purified. He is unwilling to leave you to your self-destructive ways. He knows you are your own worst enemy and that nothing makes you fall faster or harder than your love of self.

In a moment, pride may seem to revitalize. You feel empowered. Able. In this way the trap of self-sufficiency is set. Though there is no Truth in pride, your ego takes the bait.

Pride blinds to reality and its ultimate fruit is death. Death of character, death of relationship, and death of the holiness to which you are called. A forever widening gap between you and God.

Except that He intervenes.

. . .

> Everything He does is right and
> all His ways are just. And those who
> walk in pride He is able to humble.
>
> Daniel 4:37

january 23

DO YOU LOVE ME?

He asks, "Do you love me?" And God alone brings you to an honest reply of, "Yes, Lord." His presence brings you to your knees and makes you eager to ask that He teach you to love Him and to be loved by Him.

God alone moves your heart to devotion. God alone invites you. Follow Me. As you seek His presence, He presents to you relationship. You seek Him again and He brings understanding, wisdom, and discernment. Again you seek and again He responds. This is the love of God.

At the feet of Christ you are able to say, "Yes, Lord, you know that I love you." At His feet our Lord teaches you love – to love and to be loved.

. . .

Again Jesus said, "'Simon son of John, do you truly love Me?' He answered, 'Yes, Lord, You know that I love You.'"

John 21:16

AN INVITATION

Take a moment and talk with Jesus. Ask Him to make you sensitive to His presence, quick to respond to His Word. Ask Him to make His voice, His prompting, undeniable to your soul. Ask Him to be more real to you than the trees, more real than the ground on which you stand.

The presence of Christ is unlike any other, and those whose lives He has touched recognize the sound of His voice.

He invites you into His presence. Do not hesitate to sit with Him, to make the relationship a priority.

Then, regardless of circumstance, you'll recognize Christ. You will have heard Him so many times before that in the crunch you won't need to ask, "Who are you?" You'll know.

. . .

"Jesus said to them, 'Come and have breakfast.' None of the disciples dared ask Him, 'Who are You?' They knew it was the Lord."

John 21:12

UNFAILING LOVE

In a quiet moment you pour out your heart and you wait, certain you are met by the attentive ear of God.

And yet night falls, and in the dark the enemy whispers, "What if He doesn't come? What if He doesn't hear?"

What will others think if God doesn't show Himself? You wonder; you fret. You forget that when God is taken into consideration, worries must cease. You cannot worry and trust God.

You trust God because in Him there is no what if. All rests in His hands. Every word you pray reaches His ear, reaches His heart.

You trust Him for the future. He has never failed the past. This is the hope, the promise, to which you lift up your soul.

. . .

Let the morning bring me word of Your unfailing love, for I have put my trust in You. Show me the way I should go, for to You I lift up my soul.

Psalm 143:8

WHEN GOD LIMITS

Whatever natural abilities you have, they are from the Lord. Limitations, too, are from Him. You should consider them a blessing.

Limitations set by God are as much to guide as your natural abilities. They give you boundaries within which to stretch and explore.

Within boundaries you discover important aspects of your life that are key to the path God has for you. Without them you dart this way and that. You don't know where to focus your energies.

Within God-set boundaries you discover where you are meant to be more. Within His boundaries you are set free.

Even so, you remember that your abilities and your inabilities are from the Lord and for the Lord. Not for your glory, but for His.

. . .

Who makes you different from anyone else? What do you have that you did not receive? And if you did receive it, why do you boast as though you did not?

1 Corinthians 4:7

january 27

OVERCOME EVIL WITH GOOD

Too often you assume the evil to overcome is an evil outside of the self.
You forget the God transformation is
personal and individual, and one that
happens from within.

Your immediate responses throughout the
day – to people, circumstances, inconve-
niences – they reveal the nature of your
heart. In this you discover your true
attitude toward others and toward God.

Bow your head and ask God to overwhelm
your soul, to overcome all selfishness
in your heart. Ask Him to overcome your
pride with humility, your harshness
with gentleness. Ask Him to give you a
spirit that sings, even in the dark.

This very personal life change is the
light that shines. This is the curiosity
that prompts others to say, "Who is this
God?"

. . .

Do not be overcome with evil,
but overcome evil with good.

Romans 12:21

LIVE FOR THE LORD

You are invited to live your life for the Lord. You are invited to regard Him as a treasure to be sought, to covet His attentions more than you covet the attentions of any other. You are invited to lavish on Him the gift that is your life.

It is an earnest invitation to work "with all your heart, as working for the Lord," whatever your hand has found to do. You are not asked to justify your life. You are not required to find acceptance from those who cannot understand.

Justification lies with Christ. Your acceptance, too, is His.

What's more, the results are His. The fruit of a life lived honestly to God is God's alone, just as the child belongs to Him.

. . .

Whatever you do, work at it
with all your heart, as working
for the Lord, not for human masters.

Colossians 3:23

GOD HEARS

Daniel fasted and sought God for three weeks before learning he had been heard from the first day. His perseverance did not go unnoticed by God.

Like Daniel, you go before God to seek understanding. You are confident that He is a personal God; therefore, you trust that He hears, that He will answer. You trust He is compassionate and believe God when He says that He is yours and you are His.

You reach out. You seek. And you wait. You listen. You persevere.

Set your mind on God as you search for understanding. Allow your heart to be humbled by Him. Go before God, and go before Him again, always diligent, trusting your prayers are heard since the first day.

. . .

"Since the first day that you set your mind to gain understanding and to humble yourself before your God, your words were heard."

Daniel 10:12

LIFE IN HIS PRESENCE

Nothing satisfies as God does. No presence is as sweet, no protector as trustworthy, no ambition or person or desire is deep enough to fill the space that is God in your life.

You can look in all sorts of places and reach for all sorts of goals, but nothing takes the place of God. The time spent seeking Him will always be the most important and most fruitful time you spend.

Day after day you go before your Lord and He sows His life into yours. Only when you reach Eternity will you have the joy of realizing the full impact of a life lived with Him.

Lord, we live our lives with outstretched arms, reaching always for Your presence. Don't let us miss You.

. . .

"Whoever wants to save his life will lose it, but whoever loses his life for Me will find it."

Matthew 16:25

januaney 31

WORTHY OF GOD

You can't rush the sensing of God's presence. Either you wait for Him or you
do not. You are patient or impatient,
still or restless. Either you put in
the time to meet God alone or you give
up too soon. The difference is meeting
God or forever standing on the outside
looking in.

Why stand on the outside? Why give up
when the prize is God Himself?

The dynamic of a relationship with God
changes when you seek God for God alone.
When He is enough, His presence is your
desire. When your longing is to find
what pleases Him and to please Him with
all your heart.

Grant, Lord, that our motivation is
nothing less than You.

You are worthy, our Lord and God!

. . .

"You are worthy, our Lord and God, to
receive glory and honor and power, for
You created all things, and by Your will
they were created and have their being."

Revelation 4:11

The eyes of the LORD are
on those who fear Him,
on those whose hope is
in His unfailing love.

Psalm 33:18

The L<small>ORD</small> is
my strength
and my song.

Exodus 15:2

february

THE GREATEST PRIZE

Seek God for the sake of knowing Him. Search Him out. Experience His presence. Make Him the sole motive behind your Christian life. The driving force and the greatest prize. Your primary desire.

You, O God, are more than enough!

Naturally, there will be the additions. All these things. That is the promise. But all these are not properly understood or envisioned until they scarcely seem to matter. When placed next to your knowing the Almighty God, the attainment of all these becomes an afterthought. Indeed, you cannot rightly experience or know any good thing God has gifted until your heart yearns for Him above it all.

. . .

"Seek first His kingdom and His righteousness, and all these things will be given to you as well."

Matthew 6:33

FRUIT OF THE SPIRIT

There is a desire to please your Lord, and in response you are moved to give love and joy and peace. To give patience, kindness, goodness, faithfulness, gentleness, and self-control. He calls you to a life response greater than yourself, an obedience enabled and manifested by God alone. It is a way of existence that teaches you to see others more and to think of yourself less.

More than common courtesy, yours is a life of faithfulness. A life to promote peace. To show kindness when you no longer feel kind or patience when patience has run out. The fruit of a life lived with God displays itself one decision at a time as you are quietly made less and He is made more.

. . .

The fruit of the Spirit is love, joy, peace, patience, kindness, goodness, faithfulness, gentleness and self-control. Against such things there is no law.

Galatians 5:22-23

YOUR TRUE VALUE

You know what is good because God defines goodness. You know what is valued by the value placed on a thing by God. And He places value on you!

You, the valued creation, the valued child of God. The one for whose sake God reveals His glory and is making all things new.

The value system is His. It does not exist apart from Him, nor is it a system in its own right. It does not ask for the opinions or the approval of man. In this way, God exercises His own place as the most valuable of all.

Listen to His voice. He whispers your name. He identifies you. God places value on you, and by Him alone is your value revealed.

. . .

> How great is the love the Father
> has lavished on us, that we
> should be called children of God!
> And that is what we are!
>
> 1 John 3:1

A QUIET PLACE

Do not give up in your efforts to find the still, quiet place for your soul. A calm heart awaits. And a quiet mind. The soothing presence of God is in this place, and He greets you.

A little distance from the chaos of life brings perspective as all things are brought down, brought to appropriate size.

This quiet place is why God's daughters walk and do not grow weary. These moments of recharging are why we run and do not faint. In these moments God fills your cup and brings you Life.

You need rest, rest of body and rest of soul. You need time for your mind to re-focus on God. You need the opportunity to hear His voice. You need Jesus.

. . .

Those who hope in the LORD will renew their strength. They will soar on wings like eagles; they will run and not grow weary, they will walk and not be faint.

Isaiah 40:31

GOD GIVES STRENGTH

Weaknesses and struggles grant to you opportunity, time and again, to remember God is God and you are not. In the struggle, you are invited to practice living with God as your strength. Small moments of decision throughout each day.

Moments of weakness prompt you to rely on and seek God for wisdom and protection and courage. And each time God acts, you experience, yet again, proof that He is for you.

Do not wait for life to overwhelm before you choose to lean on God. Walk in His strength today. Practice it. The smaller exercises of faith build trust, and in the truly overwhelming time of need, you will find that God as your strength comes quite naturally.

. . .

He said to me, "My grace is sufficient for you, for My power is made perfect in weakness."
2 Corinthians 12:9-10

CHRIST, YOUR LIGHT

Life and the light of men. This is your Christ. So much more than an idea to consider or a time in history to debate. By Him all things are made, all life breathed, all eternity seen.

Without Him hearts lie down in darkness. Questions remain forever unanswered. The miracles of life unrevealed.

But with Him, Creation is restored. By the light that is Christ you know and understand what He has made. By His light, you know the Father and expect the Spirit.

Draw near to Him and you find all of existence is entwined in His story. His will and His ways are the key by which you experience and understand life.

Today, consider Christ. Your Light.

. . .

Through Him all things were made;
without Him nothing was made that
has been made. In Him was life, and
that life was the light of men.

John 1:3-4

GOD SEES EVERYTHING

How difficult to face the hidden self,
and how deliberate a process it must be.

In His great love, God reveals the true
self, and He presents to you redemption.
You pray, "Forgive my hidden faults,"
and by Him, what is hidden is brought
to light.

From the moment man chose himself
over God, the process, the plan of redemption, was set into motion. God is
redeeming Creation not in a sweep, but
in an unfolding. One day, one moment,
one life story at a time.

Individual stories mirror the broader
story of God, whereby all things are
made new.

Lord, forgive our hidden sins. Make them
known to us that we may turn from them,
that we may better understand ourselves
and others and You.

. . .

Who can discern his errors?
Forgive my hidden faults.

Psalm 19:12

LISTEN WELL

God's Word is a light for your soul. It is the soothing salve of your Healer and the guidepost from a Father too in love to let you go.

As you turn Scripture over in your mind, one word, then the next, remember this word is a word for you. Meditate on it carefully. The words take form, they reform, and they melt into your soul.

No corner of your life is left to darkness when spiritual ears are opened and you listen well. So consider how you listen, how you are unsatisfied with a hop and a skip through Scripture. Unsatisfied to keep a vague familiarity with your Lord.

Consider how you listen, and then watch. The Light shines in.

. . .

"Therefore consider
carefully how you listen."

Luke 8:18

BE TRUSTWORTHY

What a blessing to find yourself alongside a trustworthy person. What a relief to discover the person who holds you – your reputation, your feelings – in his or her hands suddenly proves trustworthy. A trustworthy person grants a wonderful gift. It is a gift each should delight to give others.

A gift with no strings attached and no prerequisites. Trustworthiness says, "You are safe." Trustworthiness is a form of protection. It is a lifting up and a setting free. Truly selfless, a trustworthy person considers others, and acts accordingly.

Lord, make us into a people who are trustworthy. Make us a safe place, always considering the other person. Make us for one another, where iron sharpens iron and tired shoulders find rest.

. . .

A gossip betrays a confidence, but a trustworthy person keeps a secret.

Proverbs 11:13

ALL YOUR ANXIETY

Cast your anxieties. Throw them off, each one, as they come. God is, after all, superior. His understanding surpasses all.

Seek wisdom. Seek instruction. Seek advice where you are able, where appropriate. And always cast your anxieties to the One who holds your life in His hands.

God is mindful of you, and every circumstance He can use for your good and His glory. He has not forgotten you in this trial. You are not left alone, nor to chance.

When you release uneasiness to God, you humble yourself before Him. You give Him rein to do as He sees fit. You obey as honestly as you know how, and leave the outcome and its judgment to God alone.

. . .

Cast all your anxiety on Him
because He cares for you.

1 Peter 5:7

BACK TO WHERE YOU BELONG

Was this the promise on God's heart when Adam and Eve chose themselves over Him?

God has a way of bringing His people back, of restoring the lost, sick, and broken. He is doing it now, restoring broken Creation. He has a way of never letting go and of ensuring there is always a way back.

One day life will be as intended. How sweet you will find that most precious of relationships! How sweet you will find life with your Creator, your God.

The One who, though backs have turned on Him, has never turned His back on you. Always watching over You. Wherever you go.

And carefully, completely, He is bringing you back. Back to where you belong.

. . .

"I am with you and will watch over you wherever you go, and I will bring you back to this land."

Genesis 28:15

FREELY GIVE

What has God given you? What blessings have you received? What abilities? What positions do you hold in life?

"Freely you have received," Jesus told His disciples, "freely give."

You were created by God and gifted by Him that you may give to others. Your life blessings are as much for your benefit as for the benefit of those around you.

Don't you see? You are equipped as part of a much larger whole.

So freely give with the gifts God has instilled. Ask Him to open your eyes, to make you aware of opportune moments where you are aptly blessed to be a blessing. And then, without hesitation, give. And give generously.

. . .

"Freely you have received;
freely give."

Matthew 10:8

WHERE IS YOUR HOPE?

Place your hope in the One whose Word is absolute. There is no higher authority to which you may appeal. No one can overturn the decisions of God.

Whether He heals or saves or sets free, you may go to Him in full confidence that what He grants cannot be taken away.

The Word of God is final. It is final in regards to this earth and it is final in regards to you.

And when He is the One you praise, when He is the One on which your faith lies, you can approach Him with confidence. You can go to Him and know that by Him you are loved. You are His and He is yours. No opinion can change this fact.

. . .

Heal me, O LORD, and I will be healed;
save me and I will be saved,
for You are the one I praise.

Jeremiah 17:14

HIS HEART OVERFLOWED

Jesus spoke from the overflow of His heart. He claimed to be the Son of God. He taught how to live and how to die.

You learn a great deal about your Savior when you concentrate on the heart behind His words.

Read the words Jesus spoke when He taught His disciples or healed the sick. Turn them over in your heart. Ask not only what the words mean and what they meant, but what they mean about the One who spoke them. What they mean about God. What they mean about your place before Him.

You know Him more when you face the realities of His heart.

. . .

"A tree is recognized by its fruit.
For out of the overflow
of the heart the mouth speaks."

Matthew 12:33-34

A DAY TO PRAISE!

You await the day when all things are made new, are made right. You anticipate a life unhindered by any amount of separation from God. And until that day, you acknowledge, even in its brokenness, that the earth and everything in it exists in His hands.

God has a plan of redemption for all He has made. A plan in progress that will come to great culmination. On that day you will praise Him as you have never praised Him before. All the earth will sing His name. Your praise will be pure and your praise will be perfect.

Perhaps you will scarcely recognize yourself. But all will recognize God. All will call Him King and Everlasting Lord.

. . .

Let them praise the name of the LORD,
for He commanded and they were created.

Psalm 148:5

LAMP OF THE LORD

God specializes in transforming hardship into life lessons perfectly tailored to your soul.

The struggles of life are real and are to be expected, uniquely processed by each individual child of God. He is prepared for the task.

As God sheds light on your life and your spiritual eyes are opened, start where you are. Move forward. Today. From here. Apply the lessons you have learned. Apply them today and tomorrow. One step and then the next.

He has waited for you and now is your time with Him; the time when He sheds light in dark places and refines your soul.

. . .

The lamp of the LORD searches the spirit of a man; it searches out his inmost being.

Proverbs 20:27

WHATEVER YOU DO

The tasks God gives are equal in His sight. This should encourage you and humble you deeply. What matters is the willing and obedient heart.

What task has God asked of you today? God asks for obedience and He provides the way. He does not tell you to give of someone else's harvest. He says to give of your harvest. To invest with what you have been given. Practice hearing His voice, and respond eagerly.

What appears as the least impressive may in fact be the most readily acceptable to God because of the circumstance and heart that offers it. Humble yourself before Him. Be strengthened by His grace.

Whatever God asks of you, He will provide the means and the opportunity for your servant's heart.

. . .

Whatever you do, work at it with
all your heart, as working for
the Lord, not for human masters.

Colossians 3:23

TRANSFIGURED CHRIST

There is a message for your heart and a revelation for your soul. A moment when Christ is transfigured before you, when He meets with you and you are struck with the realities of the Son of God. It isn't a child's story after all.

What will your heart do with this message? With this revelation of the Christ? Pray you are unsatisfied to observe Him from a distance. Pray for a deep desire to know Him, for an unquenchable thirst to motivate your soul.

If you are to experience Jesus honestly, you must strive to put your notions of Him aside. You must discover Him anew, refusing to measure Him by your own ideas of truth. To measure yourself by the notions of God.

. . .

"After six days Jesus took Peter, James and John with Him and led them up a high mountain, where they were all alone. There He was transfigured before them."

Mark 9:2

februari 19

A SERVANT GOD

How can ambitious minds fathom a Servant God? A crucified Christ?

At His lowest moment by earth standards, He was most obedient to the Father. He understood the cost of your restoration far better than you understand it yourself, yet was willing to bear the burden. To bear your consequence. To obey the greatest command.

Jesus did for you what you could not do for yourself. This was His righteousness and His humility.

May you be a servant, eager to do for another what he or she cannot do for him or herself, even to the point - especially to the point - of your humiliation.

. . .

"For even the Son of Man did not
come to be served, but to serve, and
to give His life as a ransom for many."

Mark 10:45

THE FREEDOM OF OBEDIENCE

Too often God's children treat sin as a good denied them rather than a danger from which they are set free. As a result, the good life offered is seldom realized. Time is wasted looking to what freedoms are believed to be lost or in denying sin altogether. Or some believe Christ's sacrifice for their eternity permits a sin-filled life on Earth.

You love the warm and exciting promises of God. Often you want words of wisdom and encouragement, not realizing "Go, and sin no more," is as liberating a phrase as, "I can do all things."

The call to obedience is a call that you may live unobstructed. When God says, "Do not sin," He says, "Discover your potential. Discover who you are."

. . .

> The man who looks intently into the
> perfect law that gives freedom, and
> continues to do this, not forgetting
> what he has heard, but doing it –
> he will be blessed in what he does.

James 1:25

february 21

NO FEAR

God has summoned you. You are the one He has redeemed. You are the one He calls His own. And though the world may be too much for you, it is never too much for Him. He is greater, so much greater, than any weight you carry or river you wade or flame you pass through.

The fearsome things in this life are never fearsome to God. They do not touch Him. They do not surprise or overwhelm Him. And when they threaten to touch you, He reaches down and takes you in His hand. He whispers to your heart, however often you need to hear, "Fear not. You are Mine."

The promise is yours. Breathe it in. Accept it as truth.

. . .

"Fear not, for I have redeemed you;
I have summoned you by name;
you are Mine."

Isaiah 43:1

THE MOUNTAINS YOU CLIMB

Mountains in life, mountains that are life, they thrill and they threaten. Stormy. Uncertain. Changing in an instant.

Life changes in an instant. And, always, the promises of God hold firm. They are remembered from the past, give courage to the future, and fortify your strength of today.

Hold steadfast to God's promises, every word He has spoken. He carries all of time while you experience one moment. And the next.

God knew this day would come. He knows your mountain. To you He makes His promises. He provides the delicate, strong, bounding feet, like the deer. The promises are yours.

. . .

The Sovereign LORD is my strength;
He makes my feet like the feet of a deer,
He enables me to tread on the heights.

Habakkuk 3:19

TO WHOM SHALL WE GO?

Once you believe and know, you do not turn back. You are moved forward, ever closer to the God who enables you to know Him. The deeper your conviction, the more you view life through the lens that is Christ. And every purpose begins to fade in comparison with knowing Him more; and every purpose illuminates at the touch of His hand.

He is your God. Do not postpone seeking Him. Do not delay in living each day by His side.

To whom shall we go? Is there another more deserving? Is there a safer place? A higher pursuit than knowing and following God? His way is life. He is life. Let nothing, no one, take the place that is His in your heart.

. . .

"Simon Peter answered Him, 'Lord, to whom shall we go? You have the words of eternal life. We believe and know that You are the Holy One of God.'"

John 6:68-69

THE LORD FULFILLS

How often have you cried, "Do not abandon me! Do not abandon the works of Your hands"? And He does not.

Your God will not abandon you. He will not lose sight of you or forget you. You, the work of His hands.

He sees your trials. He sees your frustrations. Your fears. He sees the moments that make you soar and the ones that threaten to take everything away.

Yet, you must know, God will not fail you. And you will not fail, because He never fails. He will not allow that your life should be lost.

The deep sincerity of God is forevermore. Even in the moments when you are most afraid, He is there. Working out His purpose for you. Never letting go.

. . .

The LORD will fulfill His purpose for me;
Your love, O LORD, endures forever –
do not abandon the works of Your hands.

Psalm 138:8

february 25

EXPECT GOD

You are not lost to God. The most impossible tasks, the most difficult of repentances, are possible with Him. And the most beautiful of lives have grown from the depths.

God takes your experiences and He makes you rich with a life that overflows. Nothing is pointless, nothing unusable for Him.

Do not mistake the night for His absence. Do not think He is unaware or that His purposes have been lost. That you have been lost.

Your God, He will appear. He will rain on your life and quench your thirst. All is in His hands. For you He plans good, not harm; and as surely as the sun rises He will come.

So look for Him. Expect your God who redeems.

. . .

As surely as the sun rises,
He will appear; He will come to us
like the winter rains, like the
spring rains that water the earth.

Hosea 6:3

CREATED TO KNOW HIM

No matter how feeble your step of faith, it is a step you must take. God is just and overwhelming in His might, but He is also gracious and full of compassion. Merciful. He sees straight to the heart and honors your most bumbling attempts to reach Him.

God wants you to reach Him. He has already covered the distance between you.

This God of yours is all of love. He created you to know Him in a relationship that would last for eternity.

Literal eternity.

Seek Him with your heart and your mind and your soul. Do not forfeit the greatest of relationships for which you were created. It is meant for today. It is the greatest pursuit of your life.

. . .

God did this so that men would seek Him and perhaps reach out for Him and find Him, though He is not far from each one of us. "For in Him we live and move and have our being."

Acts 17:27-28

GREATEST TREASURE

There is such beauty in a God who encourages Creation to reach out to Him and know Him. Almighty God who calls to you and says, "Hear Me. Follow Me."

Covet these still moments with Him. Seek them out. And when you find them, protect them. They are like rare gems.

He takes you by the hand and inspires you to live what matters. To see beauty in mercy, to know the necessity of justice and the unyielding strength of an honest compassion.

Close your eyes and breathe. God whispers and you see the world that He sees. Wonderful. Terrible. At once broken and restored. What is time to God?

You are with Him. Alone. And together, with every other who calls Him Lord.

. . .

"Again, the kingdom of heaven is like a merchant looking for fine pearls. When he found one of great value, he went away and sold everything he had and bought it."

Matthew 13:45-46

A HEART AT PEACE

The sudden, most unwelcome pang you feel, lay it down at Jesus' feet. You know it is envy. Thank Him for your blessings and for the blessings He grants to others. Thank Him that He is at work in every life. To each He grants a special purpose and plan.

This twinge is at once unexpected and too often ignored. You do not want to acknowledge envy, but call it out. Let it go. It does not belong to you. It does not belong on you. But it will absolutely drag you down.

Envy will pin you in the dirt and make you lose site of who you are. Throw it at once from you and praise your God!

. . .

A heart at peace gives life to the body, but envy rots the bones.

Proverbs 14:30

FAITH MADE REAL

The Christian life is a process whereby you learn about yourself and you learn about God. You choose daily, one decision at a time, your ways or God's ways. And, whatever the outcome, the next day the process continues. If you failed yesterday, you may succeed today.

The process of learning an instrument is what makes a musician. The process of being a parent is where parenting is learned. The process of the Christian life is where you learn to be Christian.

Each is in process. Today brings success and failures. The getting up, the moving forward, the knowing you are forgiven and learning to lean on God. Consistency. Perseverance. The never giving up. This is where you begin, where faith is made real.

. . .

You see that his faith and his actions were working together, and his faith was made complete by what he did.

James 2:22

The LORD replied, "My Presence
will go with you, and I
will give you rest."

Exodus 33:14

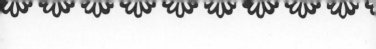

Give thanks to the
LORD, for He is
good; His love
endures forever.

1 Chronicles 16:34

march

GRACE AND WORKS

God's grace saves, and His grace prompts the work of your hands. This is why you cannot have one without the other, grace without works. Grace stirs the good work and the work reflects the grace.

Thank God for His generous grace! His grace saves and escorts you to the life He offers. Grace is life eternal, direct from the hand of God.

Thank Him, too, for the good works grace enables. Pray you do not overshadow grace with works or works with grace, but that God will bring you to an understanding of how one necessarily compliments the other.

There is great beauty in knowing you are the work of God's hand. Freedom in knowing He is not the work of yours.

. . .

Because of His great love for us, God, who is rich in mercy, made us alive with Christ even when we were dead in transgressions — it is by grace you have been saved.

Ephesians 2:4-5

YOU ALONE, O LORD

Open your eyes and consider all God has made. The waves are at His command. The stars shine because He makes it so. Flowers bloom and He sees them, every one.

Consider your great, great God and allow your heart to swell with adoration for His name.

You can lie down and sleep in peace. There is no one like your God. He sets the sun and provides rest for His children. Rest for your soul.

God is great! Grant Him the joy of hearing praise from your lips. Grant Him the satisfaction of your peace of mind, of a child that knows she sleeps in safety so long as she sleeps in the care of her Lord.

. . .

I will lie down and sleep in peace,
    for You alone, O LORD,
    make me dwell in safety.

Psalm 4:8

WHEN YOU FAIL

There are times when God allows failure so that He may present a new opportunity. If Peter had had a successful night fishing, he may not have been as overwhelmed when Jesus filled the nets (Luke 5:5-6). He may not have been as quick to drop everything to follow Christ.

Your ways do not compare with God's, yet you have a knack for overestimating yourself and underestimating what He offers.

But God's love transcends every inflated ego. In His mercy He takes you to the end of yourself, to a place where you are able to choose Him honestly and wholehearted.

He knows He is your life source. And He knows temporal failure is a cost often worth paying.

. . .

"Then Jesus said to Simon, 'Don't be afraid; from now on you will catch men.' So they pulled their boats up on shore, left everything and followed Him."

Luke 5:10-11

SLOW DOWN

Slow down.

God has a word for you, but He needs you
to stop thinking so fast, dreaming so
fast, and listening so fast. He needs you
to pray deep prayers that come from a soul
thirsty to be quenched by God.

He needs you to meditate on His Word.
Scripture is available that you might know
God more. Do not neglect it.

Find a quiet place and rest. This is your
time to recharge. This is your time to remember how to listen for God's voice. You
heard Him when you were a child. Hear Him
now.

Slow down. Hear. Rest. Be refreshed by
the beautiful presence of your perfect
Savior. He renews and makes you ready for
the day to come.

. . .

"Because so many people were coming
and going that they did not even
have a chance to eat, He said to
them, 'Come with Me by yourselves to
a quiet place and get some rest.'"

Mark 6:31

NO OTHER

Do not mistake the effects of God for God
Himself, setting sight on the healing
over the Healer or the blessings over
the One who blesses.

Faith purposefully placed in God un-
leashes the spiritual power whereby you
experience all healing, blessing, and
spiritual understanding. You are given
these things by your Father, but not as
a replacement for His presence.

God alone saves. Without Him, nothing
you seek is available. Without God, you
cease, even, to exist.

Seek Him because He is God. Remind yourself that Christ is the ultimate blessing and your final destination. Let
nothing come between you. Let your heart
crave nothing more than it craves the
presence of the Father, the Son, and the
Spirit.

. . .

"Turn to Me and be saved, all
you ends of the earth; for
I am God, and there is no other."

Isaiah 45:22

YOU WILL SEE

It is not uncommon to see faults in others before admitting to faults of your own. You know you are the student, God the teacher. Yet you find yourself eager to run ahead. You ask, "What about him? What about his faults?"

"But everyone who is fully trained will be like his teacher ... then you will see clearly."

You begin to see clearly as you become more like the Teacher. The faults of others are not as you thought. Life requires greater sacrifice than anticipated, and deep, deep empathy.

Then you see the cost – the cross – and are overwhelmed, made weak by the realization of the price once paid. Quite suddenly you begin to grasp the overwhelming enormity of the love He grants, and the love He requires.

. . .

"Can a blind man lead a blind man? ... but everyone who is fully trained will be like his teacher ... first take the plank out of your eye, and then you will see clearly."

Luke 6:39-42

GOD RESTORES THE BROKEN

God has a way of healing His wayward
child. He does not hold sins against His
own. He draws you near. He restores.

If God willed condemnation, Jesus
needn't have come. Man would have pun-
ished himself by the consequences of
sin. No, God does not desire punishment,
but healing.

Go to God and He rolls up His sleeves.
He has been waiting for this moment of
return, and He sets to work as only He
can. God forgives and disciplines. He
teaches. He lifts you up and says, "Now,
try again."

Do not shy away from God's love. Instead,
confess everything. He is eager and
waiting to hear you say, "Not my will,
Lord. Teach me Yours."

He gave His Son for this moment.

. . .

"I will heal their waywardness
and love them freely, for My
anger has turned away from them."

Hosea 14:4

CHOOSE HIM

There is a difference between the person who yields and the person who chooses. The person who yields may walk blindly, either from unexamined principles or surrounding influences. The person who deliberately chooses has weighed the evidence, the options, and weighed the price. She is the one who will not look back when her hand is to the plow (Luke 9:62).

When at once you have chosen Christ, you may then properly yield to His Word; but if you have not first chosen, you will never find the strength in you to yield. Not when the yielding matters. Christ deliberately chose you. Choose Him.

And when you have chosen, the journey of discipleship begins. Christ leads the way.

. . .

"Choose for yourselves this day whom you will serve."

Joshua 24:15

LEARNING TO LIVE

You cannot fake the Spirit of Christ, but you do know what it looks like.

A righteous heart surprises with its holy sincerity. It remains in Truth when the rest are exposed. And so you recognize the truly pure, considerate heart.

Often you are stunned to discover what you believed was Christ in you was nothing more than your own attempts to clean the outside of the cup. The dying to the self, the becoming less that He might be more, proves a tedious process. None are born righteous.

To pick up your cross, then, proves a daily business, mostly because you dropped it the day before.

. . .

The wisdom that comes from heaven is first of all pure; then peace-loving, considerate, submissive, full of mercy and good fruit, impartial and sincere. Peacemakers who sow in peace raise a harvest of righteousness.

James 3:17-18

A MINDFUL GOD

How lovely to know you do not reach for God in vain. Nor do you seek the attention of One with no recollection of you.

God could have created a world in which he paid little notice. He could have made you and neglected to prompt you to seek His face. But He didn't.

God created you and in you He has a personal interest. When you pray, you pray because God first put the idea into your mind. When you listen for Him, it is only because He has first whispered to your heart.

You would not know to seek Him if He had not sought you first. For this reason you approach God with confidence. He wants to be found.

. . .

What is man that You are mindful of him, the son of man that You care for him? You made him a little lower than the heavenly beings and crowned him with glory and honor.

Psalm 8:4-5

SPIRITUALLY DISCERNED

There are some able to accept the ways of God and there are some, it seems, who are unable. What are you to do when you find you are not as spiritually discerning as you hoped?

What limits the knowledge God reveals to a soul? What limits spiritual growth? Spiritual understanding?

Lord, clear the path from us to You. Do not let us stand in the way. This is not a journey we can manage on our own.

We want to know and see clearly the beauty of Your ways. To know the secrets that only You reveal.

Cleanse us and heal us. Be the One who enables us to see the face of God. To see You.

. . .

The man without the Spirit does not accept the things that come from the Spirit of God, for they are foolishness to him, and he cannot understand them, because they are spiritually discerned.

1 Corinthians 2:14

FOUND BY GOD

You are never too lost to be found by God or so far gone that He does not want you back. In your most vulnerable and stubborn states, He waits and watches for your return.

This God who invites you into the company of Heaven, He is famous for forgiveness. He is the giver of second chances and third chances and seventy times seven chances, the first to throw open His arms to welcome you home.

Your God is the Father who sees the potential in you that no one else sees. No matter how much you may have been loved on this earth, God loves you more. And He will never leave you and He can never be taken away.

. . .

"'For this son of mine was dead and is
alive again; he was lost and is found.'
So they began to celebrate."

Luke 15:24

A LIMITLESS GOD!

God knows your limitations. Your limited experience, knowledge, faith. He knows where to stretch you and where to protect you. What is more, your limits are nothing to God's abilities. In fact, when your life is grounded in the realities of God, all limits dissolve.

On your own and left to your own purposes, you will always be limited by your self. However, when you pour yourself out daily to God and His purposes you find all limits cease. At this point the responsibility lies with Him alone. He is the One responsible for your life and its direction. You are responsible for seeking God.

So do not fuel your ego by focusing on your limitations. Even this is pride. Rather, fuel faith. Fuel Truth.

. . .

Now to Him who is able to do immeasurably more than all we ask or imagine, according to His power that is at work within us, to Him be glory in the church and in Christ Jesus throughout all generations, for ever and ever! Amen.

Ephesians 3:20-21

TAKE HEART

By Christ you conquer life's trials. His ability fuels you, and by Him you find all confidence and wisdom.

Because of Christ, you do not need to be overwhelmed by the spiritual and physical battles you face. But when you rely on yourself, on your abilities or the abilities of others, you are made afraid and vulnerable.

Without God you are weak, because He is the only true source for strength. He is your protector and the reason for lasting hope.

The journey will not always be easy, but in Christ you are guaranteed it will be victorious.

. . .

"I have told you these things, so
that in Me you may have peace.
In this world you will have trouble.
But take heart!
I have overcome the world."

John 16:33

BE KIND

Today, look for ways to show kindness. An opportunity to be kind is often right under your nose, but you fail to see it. Or you underestimate the impact it may have on a life.

But kindness is of enormous importance! Kindness shown is an act of faith. It is obedience and it is love.

Take Jesus at His Word when He says the smallest act of kindness is an act given to Himself.

Mary was able to bless Jesus in person when she anointed Him with perfume. Today, the most direct path to blessing Christ is to bless those He loves. Think of the ones you love and how pleased you are when someone shows them kindness.

. . .

"The King will reply, 'I tell you the truth, whatever you did for one of the least of these brothers of Mine, you did for Me.'"

Matthew 25:40

REUNITED IN GOD

Embrace today with the joy of one whose living God is on her side!

There was a time when you were an enemy to God. You turned your back on Him because you loved yourself in His place. Yet even then He had a plan for forgiveness and re-conciliation. God does not want enemies.

Now, because of Christ, you are reunited to God. He sees sons and daughters. Family.

If God was good to you when you denied Him, planning and sacrificing even His Son for your future, think what wonderful blessings He must have for you now that you are His own! Think what goodness is in store now that your future is not set against Him, but for Him. And with Him.

. . .

For if, while we were God's enemies,
we were reconciled to Him through
the death of His Son, how much more,
having been reconciled, shall
we be saved through His life!

Romans 5:10

BELIEVE HIM

You are not a stranger to God. He has always known everything about you. How you look. How you feel. What plans He has for you, what dreams for your heart. That is why He made you. Because He wanted you.

And He knew your future from the moment He knew your name. He is, in fact, already there. Time is not the same for God as for you. His vision is not limited, like yours, to past experience. The future is as the present to God.

That is why you can believe Him when He says He is faithful. You trust the promised refuge of His wings because it is not a promise for what may be; it is a promise for what is.

. . .

He will cover you with His feathers, and under His wings you will find refuge; His faithfulness will be your shield and rampart.

Psalm 91:4

PERFECT LOVE

One of the wonderful gifts Christ offers
is the call to perfection. This is not to
say you reach perfection on earth. All of
Creation is in a sinful state. Perfection
today seems impossible. Yet even so,
Christ calls you to it.

What He means is not that He wants you
to be something you are not, but that He
wants you to be as He intended from the
first, before the Fall.

And He will have His way, if you let Him.
Of course, the perfection intended by God
can only be brought about by God Himself.
And this is exactly what Christ is doing.
He repairs the broken.

One day you will wake up restored. Perfect.
And all because of the perfect love of
God.

. . .

"Be perfect, therefore, as your
heavenly Father is perfect."

Matthew 5:48

GOD ANCHORS YOU

God is forever committed to your well-being. You can trust the promises of His Word. You can trust that He is committed to your salvation and to your becoming every bit the child of God you were created to be.

This is the love of God, and the hope He provides is an anchor for your soul. Even in the midst of uncertainty you can keep on keeping on, trusting and believing Mighty God is on your side.

He is in the struggle and holds you steadfast. The outcome, remember, is His. Your life resides in His hands. Nothing is too much for Him. Nothing a surprise.

He will pick you up when you stumble and rescue you from the storm.

. . .

> We have this hope as an anchor
> for the soul, firm and secure.
>
> Hebrews 6:19

CONSTANT COMMUNION

Your time with God does not end when you say, "Amen." It continues. Your whole life is one long visit with Him. Each day a page in the story.

This is your most precious of relationships. No need to fill the silence. No need to speak a word. For you, there is an open invitation to sit at the feet of Christ. To choose daily the better thing.

In this way of being together, you develop a habit of constant communication with God. You go about your day in unbroken communion with Him.

Your spirit is kept in prayer all day long. It makes work worship and opens your eyes to life's tiny glimpses of God's glory.

. . .

Guide me in Your truth and teach me,
for You are God my Savior,
and my hope is in You all day long.

Psalm 25:5

LIVE FOR TODAY

Your eternity is redeemed. For you, death is no longer a concern. To leave this world means to enter completely and finally into that most perfect of unions with your Lord.

Let Him also redeem your present. If death was not too much for God, then neither are the blunders of your past. He even promises to use those blunders, every one of them, for His glory.

There can be no greater, no holier, opportunity than one which brings God glory. And how glorified He will be when He transforms your life on earth! He delights to do this for you. It is just one more step that draws you closer to Him. And close is where He wants you to be.

· · ·

We were therefore buried with Him
through baptism into death in order that,
just as Christ was raised from the
dead through the glory of the Father,
we too may live a new life.

Romans 6:4

NO FEAR IN LOVE

Do not give in when fear threatens to over-whelm your soul. Rather, remember God's promises. Name them and claim them. Speak the Truth, regardless of how you feel.

Use the opportunity to prove your faith and to grow in faithfulness. Fear says you are alone and vulnerable, but Truth says God will never leave you nor forsake you.

Fear invites you to live by your own means, while God invites you to live in the protection of His will. You are never alone.

In Christ there is no fear. His love drives out fear and drives you to a faith un-shakable. When you feel afraid, take your fears to God. Take fear to Him again and again. He will not fail you.

. . .

There is no fear in love.
But perfect love drives out fear.
1 John 4:18

THE GIFT OF GOD'S WORD

In God's Word you find truth of every kind. Truth about God and truth about yourself. Truth about all of creation. At times the realities of this two edged sword threaten to overwhelm you, but God is the shield. You see that, too, when you delve into His Word.

And what a lovely gift! A personal word to remind you that God is God. He is for you. He wants to be known by you.

God's Word is a living word. You read it to know Him more and in turn you find that His Word knows you.

Scripture reveals God to you and then it reveals you to you. It is like seeing yourself for the very first time.

. . .

Every word of God is flawless; He is a shield to those who take refuge in Him.

Proverbs 30:5

GOD KNOWS THE WAY

God knows your destination. Between the two of you, He is the One who has seen it and been there. And He is the One who knows the way.

Take God's hand and trust as He leads. Allow Him to connect the dots of all your life experiences. He knows the value of each one, and He has ordained their working together.

Whether or not you see it today, God has a plan and a purpose for your life. This plan unfolds in the day to day activities. Focus continually on God and live the journey. Trust Him to navigate. God knows you better than you know yourself. He searches you and molds you. He holds you close. Your job is to know Him more.

. . .

If I rise on the wings of the dawn,
if I settle on the far side of the sea,
even there Your hand will guide me,
Your right hand will hold me fast.

Psalms 139:9-10

HIS LOVE IS FOREVER

There is no place you can go where God is not present. Spiritually, physically, and mentally, God is there to see all and hear your inmost thoughts.

This God of yours, He is relentless in His love for you. And His love is ever-lasting, the kind of love that never gives up and always gives all.

It is the kind of love that seeks you out. God's love waits for and calls to you. It is a deep, mature love, more than is comprehensible. A greater commitment than any can fathom.

It is a love that humbles and brings you to your knees. Who are you that God should love you so? He creates you and shapes you and invites you into His presence.

. . .

Give thanks to the LORD, for He is good;
His love endures forever.

1 Chronicles 16:34

GOD WILL REJOICE!

Commit yourself to God and you will see how He delights in you. The Creator of the universe will rejoice over you with singing!

Just imagine! All powerful God. Rejoicing. Over you!

You have yet to know the ultimate freedom that will come from surrendering your life completely to Him. But one day all will come to fruition. God's children will be swept up to Him where He will take great delight and quiet you with His love.

Everything not of God will fall away. Wrongs will be set right. And you will be purified in His love, no longer separated from Him by this world. Your God is merciful!

Merciful and good and mighty to save!

. . .

> The LORD your God is with you, He is mighty to save. He will take great delight in you, He will quiet you with His love, He will rejoice over you with singing.
>
> Zephaniah 3:17

CLOSE THE DOOR

There is no substitute for time spent alone with God. The moments of your day carved out for listening to Him and praising Him and studying His Word are the moments of your day that build the foundations of your life. These are the moments on which all else hinges. These are the moments when you meet God.

Protect this time. Cherish it. Develop it. Never neglect it. God placed a need in your life for Him. When you nurture this relationship you nurture every aspect of your day-to-day. Your family, your friends, your job, the people you care about need you to care about God. They need you to draw close to Him and allow Him to draw close to you.

. . .

"When you pray, go into your room, close the door and pray to your Father, who is unseen. Then your Father, who sees what is done in secret, will reward you."

Matthew 6:6

A GOD OF LAUGHTER

The truth about God is that He redeems what you thought was lost, and in this promise your spirit soars.

Times of waiting are necessary. Here you learn perseverance and trust. His ways are the best ways. And when His promises are fulfilled, you look back and see He was always in control.

God makes you laugh when He accomplishes in you what you never thought possible. In His hands you are proof of the good God you serve.

Whatever your limitations, these are only that you may come to fully appreciate God's hand in your life. You need daily reminders that you are not enough and God in you is essential. Praise Him in your weakness. Praise Him in promises fulfilled!

. . .

"Sarah said, 'God has brought me laughter, and everyone who hears about this will laugh with me.'"

Genesis 21:6

SIMPLY ASK

When faced with difficulties, it is easy to feel you are trapped within a downward spiral. All face hardships and the consequences of poor decisions made. But God says all can be saved!

Joel spoke to people who had made many wrong decisions in their lives and toward God. He taught them about their current condition and about the future condition of Israel. And he reminded them that their God was a God of restoration.

Your God is the very same. He restores your eternity and restores your present. All you need to do is ask. As you go about your day, call on God for help and direction. You can trust in the permanence of His faithfulness. You can trust Him for today and for forever.

. . .

Everyone who calls on the
name of the LORD will be saved.

Joel 2:32

A HELPING HAND

You may not have the gift of physical healing like Peter, but in some way God has given you an ability to take another by the hand and help her to stand.

Jesus' work on earth is not done. He continues to reveal Himself and to work in and through the lives of those who call on Him. He is alive and even today He heals this broken world.

Ask God to help you see the needs of others. And whatever help He provides them through you, remember it is a help by Christ and Christ alone. Give Him the glory every time. Pride is a nuisance to be forever kept in check.

. . .

Taking him by the right hand, he
helped him up, and instantly the
man's feet and ankles became strong.

Acts 3:7

PRACTICE TRUSTING GOD

Do not be surprised when God allows trials in your life. Trusting God takes patience and practice, and He is building your faith. He is teaching you how to fully rely on Him.

If God did not allow times to practice trust, you would be like a withering tree planted in the desert. Trials grow deep faith roots. Roots that reach the water.

God is here for you. He does not leave your life to chance, nor is He satisfied to leave you in an infant state. He wants to mature you. The world needs fruitful trees in this thirsty land.

God is giving you trust lessons, so lean on Him when you are afraid and unsure. Your confidence in Him will grow and anchor your soul.

. . .

"Blessed is the man who trusts in the LORD, whose confidence is in Him. He will be like a tree planted by the water that sends out its roots by the stream."

Jeremiah 17:7-8

By day the LORD directs
His love, at night
His song is with me –
a prayer to the
God of my life.

Psalm 42:8

Let us hold
unswervingly to the hope
we profess, for He who
promised is faithful.

Hebrews 10:23

april

OAKS OF RIGHTEOUSNESS

God desires to make His people a display of His splendor. The display is left to God, but what you do with His Word and what you do with His presence is of great importance.

Your individual relationship with God shapes the church.

Concern yourself with what goes into your soul and God will concern Himself with what comes out. Be always aware of what your eyes see and what your ears hear. Take note of what you allow your mind to ponder.

He sees every believer, the individual parts of a greater whole. He prunes. He shapes. He tends. He grows you into the kingdom of Heaven.

Therefore, concern yourself with His presence and trust the collective out-come to Him.

. . .

They will be called oaks of righteousness, a planting of the LORD for the display of His splendor.

Isaiah 61:3

LOVE HIM

When you are honest, you may find you want to be loved by God while you yourself do little to love Him in return. You approach Him with needs and wants and desires.

You approach Him on behalf of others. You approach Him because you know how desperately you need Him. But if you will have Him at all, you must love Him above all else.

You must love God in a way that makes knowing Him more important than the requests you make. The more you love Him, the more you will trust Him. And the more you are apt to accept His will above your own, the better you will understand why loving God means loving others before yourself.

. . .

"Know therefore that the LORD your God is God; He is the faithful God, keeping His covenant of love to a thousand generations of those who love Him and keep His commands."

Deuteronomy 7:9

GOD, YOUR FRIEND

Do you meet with God alone? Do you find a quiet place? He will speak with you, as with a friend; and He will bring you to your knees as you come to know the glory that is God. But you must be willing to seek and you must be willing to listen.

The conversation between man and God began at the beginning of time and you are invited to take part, to know Him. It is a conversation at once initiated and directed by God Himself, and it invites you into relationship with the Creator of all.

Do not miss the opportunity to know your God. Let Him speak into your life. Let Him reveal to you His heart and His glory.

. . .

The LORD would speak to
Moses face to face, as a
man speaks with his friend.

Exodus 33:11

GOD STRETCHES YOU

God knows you. He loves you. And if you are willing, He will stretch you past your here and now. He will move you to a place where you are able to do, perceive, become, and understand more than you thought possible.

From the beginning of time God has prepared a place and a way for you. He has always been the One willing to move heaven and earth on your behalf. He has always been the One – the only One – able to do so.

Allow Him to be your wisdom and your ultimate motivation, your one heart's desire. Make God the director of your life and then sit in His presence. Listen. Worship. And let the stirring of His Spirit speak life into your soul.

. . .

This is my prayer: that your love may abound more and more in knowledge and depth of insight, so that you my be able to discern what is best and may be pure and blameless until the day of Christ.

Philippians 1:9-10

PRESS ON

When you constantly look at what you are not, where you are not, and who you are not, you miss the moments to be lived today and now. All your looking back keeps you from moving forward in life and in your faith.

You have questions and they often make you feel ill fit, but God already has the answers. You do not know what He has planned for your life. And since you cannot know, all this self-centered introspection is a pointless distraction.

When you find yourself drifting into self-pity, reorient your thoughts. Take time to worship God. Recite His Word to yourself throughout the day. Lay every thought aside except His glorious name. You will soon find His promised peace.

. . .

Not that I have already obtained all this, or have already been made perfect, but I press on to take hold of that for which Christ Jesus took hold of me.

Philippians 3:12

NECESSARY REPENTANCE

Do not be afraid of the shame that leads to repentance. Repentance is necessary if you will see grace at work or experience life renewed. Repentance is necessary for you to come to any amount of understanding regarding the cross.

Forgiveness means very little prior to repentance, both in the forgiveness you receive and the forgiveness you give. The price Christ paid may even seem unnecessary.

But an honest repentance takes you to your knees. It brings you to a place where you are able to see, at last, the truth about Christ. And when you go to Him, Christ accepts your repentance. He takes away your shame. He makes all things new.

Repentance helps you understand God more.

. . .

The Lord is not slow in keeping
His promise, as some understand
slowness. He is patient with you,
not wanting anyone to perish, but
everyone to come to repentance.

2 Peter 3:9

A SHIELD AROUND YOU

Thank God and praise His name because He never leaves your life to chance. God answers those who seek Him. He grants wisdom to those who ask. He grows His children into spiritual maturity.

God opens doors He sees fit to open and He closes doors He sees fit to close. You can trust God with your life. Praise Him because of this. Praise Him because nothing in your life was a surprise to Him. He is prepared for every day.

What is more, God is a constant shield around you. He sees you through. He lifts up your head and makes you a glory and a testament to Him.

You are safe even in the midst of uncertainty, because of God's constant hand.

· · ·

But You are a shield around me,
O LORD; You bestow glory
on me and lift up my head.

Psalm 3:3

TO BELONG TO CHRIST

What a relief to know you answer to God
alone! To the One who loves you more than
any other is capable.

He looks on you, His child, and takes
you as His responsibility and His great
joy. Christ will not see you condemned.
He delights to set you free and give you
life.

On the day of judgment, Christ provides
both the question and the answer. He is
your justification. Because He is enough,
He makes you enough.

If you are bound to Christ you are bound
by nothing else. You are free because you
have chosen the safety of being God's
alone.

What can harm you when God stands in the
gap? Who can judge those approved by the
highest authority?

. . .

If I were still trying to please men,
I would not be a servant of Christ.

Galatians 1:10

BE FAITHFUL

What God has given in life, He gives with the instruction that you learn to invest. Whether relationships, talents, opportunities to serve, whatever God has placed in your path, you may consider them as blessings to be cared for and tended. Blessings to be invested in God's church and in the relationship you have with Him. Life is full of talents that belong to the Master. He expects a good return.

You do not always know what to expect in the return. But you can trust the process to refine you and make you more each day to reflect Christ.

Today, take inventory of your life and all that is in it. Remember to invest your life as one expecting Christ's return.

. . .

"His master replied, 'Well done, good and faithful servant! You have been faithful with a few things; I will put you in charge of many things. Come and share your master's happiness!'"

Matthew 25:23

HYMNS AT MIDNIGHT

God is developing in you a faith that sings at midnight! It is a faith that cannot be explained as mere optimism or maturity or having the right attitude. It is a faith that will send you soaring when by all accounts you should be sinking.

This faith is God centered. It waits on Him. Listens for Him. Pursues Him. It praises His name because it knows that when hardships come, God is prepared to shine.

Others are listening. They remember what you have said about God in the past. But for you, their faces slip away in the night. You do not see them. You see God.

These times are difficult, but they solidify the faith you have spent years nurturing and praying for.

. . .

About midnight Paul and Silas were praying and singing hymns to God, and the other prisoners were listening to them.

Acts 16:25

THE LORD IS GOOD

God has provided a life in which you are invited to partake. A good life. A life you are encouraged to taste and see. A life where God presents to you a sample of what eternity brings.

Often, though, you are distracted by the evil in this world. You focus on the problems and even blame God or doubt Him because of them.

The evil in this world is simply because God has not been allowed His rightful place in Creation. In foolishness, humanity separates itself from God and then blames Him for what that separation brings. Every life needs God in increasing measure.

Where God is allowed, there is great goodness. There is great joy and hope.

. . .

Taste and see that
the LORD is good.

Psalm 34:8

LIVE BY THE SPIRIT

By Christ's atonement, you are saved to life and the Holy Spirit is available to you.

If you want to experience life as led by the Spirit, put the faculty to use. Practice listening and stepping out. You will find God proves His ability to be heard and obeyed.

By the Spirit you learn to make decisions. You learn to test what you believe God is sharing with your heart. When a door closes, you accept it as His guidance. With each step you become more familiar with His voice.

There is more to knowing God than intellect. The experience of life with Him comes in the day to day practice of His presence, in your willingness to set your knowledge of Him to motion.

· · ·

"The Spirit gives life; the flesh counts for nothing. The words I have spoken to you are spirit and they are life."

John 6:63

DO YOU BELIEVE?

Do you believe you are God's own? Do you believe, truly, that He chose you and loves you? That He has a special place in His story for you?

Your own disbelief and your lack of assurance in God's intentions toward you hold you back from the life He offers. Often you do not even realize the doubt you hold in your heart. It stems from a doubt you have in yourself, that you are not quite good enough.

Low self-esteem is a camouflage for pride. It is also disbelief. It doubts what God will do.

Trust God. Believe Him when He says He is for you.

Today, search your heart. Do you believe God is on your side? That He chose you?

. . .

"For I know the plans I have for you," declares the LORD, "plans to prosper you and not to harm you, plans to give you hope and a future."

Jeremiah 29:11

BE TRANSFORMED

Do not be surprised when God reveals a new perspective of Himself to you. Test the revelation against Scripture. He never changes and His Word is given as a means to know Him.

Often as you patiently draw near to God, you discover He is not as you thought. This is good. It means you are coming to know the truths about God and not trusting a made up version of Him.

And when you have tested the revelation and found it to be true, test yourself against it. Test your words and attitudes and actions.

Seek God for the sake of knowing Him more, for the sake of seeing Him clearer today than yesterday. He waits for you. He makes what is invisible seen.

. . .

Do not conform any longer to the pattern of this world, but be transformed by the renewing of your mind. Then you will be able to test and approve what God's will is – His good, pleasing and perfect will.

Romans 12:2

GOD'S LOVE

Nothing can separate you from God's love. His love is forever, in good times and bad. And Christ is there, too, interceding on your behalf.

God's love for you is manifest daily in the actions of Christ. Christ interceded in your death and He intercedes for you now in life.

The work Christ accomplished in His crucifixion is a work that brings everything to perfect completion. This includes you, and nothing – nothing – can separate you from the One whose joy it is to see you complete.

Because of this constant and perfect intercession, you can address God with confidence. Your God both hears and provides the prayer; because when you do not know what to pray, even then Christ intercedes, speaking on your behalf.

· · ·

Neither height nor depth, nor anything
else in all creation, will be able
to separate us from the love of God
that is in Christ Jesus our Lord.

Romans 8:39

YOU ARE A TEMPLE

However awesome the idea may seem, you are a temple, and God has chosen for the Holy Spirit to dwell inside of you. God makes Himself present in your life. He makes you holy by His own holiness, righteous by His righteousness.

When you are alert to God's presence, you are alert to the experiences of God in and on your life. And as you observe His works, you become more apt to accept and put into practice any life change He requires.

God is always present. In the awareness of His presence your relationship with Him is made personal. He takes your hand in the day to day and you eagerly search for Him there.

Be always aware of Him. He is your God.

. . .

> Do you not know that your body is a temple of the Holy Spirit, who is in you, whom you have received from God? You are not your own.

1 Corinthians 6:19

LOVE MORE

God will never look at you and say, "If only she would learn to love a little less."

You never need to worry that you care too much or that you're too merciful or too forgiving. The answer will always be no. You are not. You never run the risk of loving too much, only of loving too seldom.

You do run the risk of underestimating love or misunderstanding it, or defining it incorrectly. You run the risk of not knowing how to accept love from the One who offers it so perfectly.

You run the risk of never bowing your head to ask God to teach the value of real, honest love.

There is a lot of talk about love. Pray for understanding.

. . .

May the Lord make your love increase and overflow for each other and for everyone else.

1 Thessalonians 3:12

TEST ME IN THIS

Your God, He knows everything about you. He knows where you struggle. He knows what you ignore. He knows the areas in life where you lack knowledge and the areas where you thirst.

And He is the only One able to fill your cup. This God you claim, He looks you in the face and says, "Bow down to Me." And you cringe, because you bow to no one.

But God, He knows everything about you. He commands that you bow because He is Almighty, and because without Him He knows you meet only death.

Hold nothing back from Him and He will hold nothing back from you.

If you feel like you are walking in mud, it may be that you have not learned to kneel.

. . .

"Test Me in this," says the LORD Almighty,
"and see if I will not throw
open the floodgates of heaven."

Malachi 3:10

ONE CAME BACK

Be the one who goes back. Be the one who falls at Jesus' feet and says, "I see who You are! I see what You have done. Let me follow You! Let me thank You every single day with my life."

Christ has saved so many who never do look back. They accept the freedom but do not understand the cost. They do not see clearly what Christ has done.

Pray to God that your heart will not be so blind. Ask Him to help you realize, to help you understand, what was at stake.

Search our hearts, O God! Do not leave us in darkness. Do not leave us unaware of the weighty price You paid to call us Your own. Forgive us.

Thank You!

· · ·

"One of them, when he saw he was healed, came back, praising God in a loud voice."

Luke 17:15

BELIEVE GOD

Abraham believed, though he did not know where he was going. He did not have to know. God knew.

God knew the details, and God's omniscience was enough. Abraham chose more than a belief in God, a belief that God existed. Abraham chose faith. He chose to believe in God and also to believe God – that God would do what He said He would do.

Abraham knew he served a sufficient God. A God who did not require self-sufficiency on part of His children, because He Himself was and is sufficient enough.

Test your beliefs, your actions, against Scripture and see whether you are selective in your belief about God, whether you merely believe in Him or whether you believe God Himself.

. . .

By faith Abraham, when called to go to
a place he would later receive as his
inheritance, obeyed and went, even though
he did not know where he was going.

Hebrews 11:8

NOW THAT YOU SEE

What will you do, when your spiritual eyes have seen God? When you no longer only hear of Him, but have come to face the truth of Him? Will you be the same, or will you allow your life to be different tomorrow than it is today because of the reality of Him?

God meant for ears to hear of Him and eyes, in turn, to see. He meant that hearts would face Him. And the question now is what will you do?

When you have at once gone from hearing about God to hearing from God, you have to make a choice. You have come to a place of seeing Him. Pray today that nothing will impair your view.

. . .

My ears had heard of You but
now my eyes have seen You.

Job 42:5

HE BECOMES GREATER

In your efforts to know God, you often begin with all attentions on the I. You build yourself up, either in your own eyes or in the eyes of others. Intentionally or not, you feed your pride and misunderstand your place in God's story.

No matter. In the midst of the mess you continue to seek God and He sets the course. He allows you to face yourself each day as He sees fit. He makes you aware and opens your eyes to who you are, to who He is, and to the realities of a life reflective of Christ.

The journey is slow and deliberate. As God opens your spiritual eyes, you begin to turn. One day you find yourself proclaiming, as did John.

. . .

"He must become greater;
I must become less."

John 3:30

MOMENTS WITH GOD

Private prayers are personal moments God spends with you alone. No other is present. No one else hears. When His presence manifests, it is for your heart and none other.

You pray, "Listen," and He does. You pray, "Hear my voice." He does. And when you wait in expectation, God responds.

God is with you in every word you pray. These moments are not lost and they are not in vain. They build a bond between you and God that is for all eternity.

One day you will see His face. You will recognize Him and you will know at once He recognizes you too. In that moment you will know there is nothing more natural than this perfect relationship between you and God.

. . .

Listen ... for to You I pray.
In the morning, O LORD, You hear my voice;
... I wait in expectation.

Psalm 5:2-3

HE MAKES WITNESSES

Your hardships are important.

When you ask or make a promise to serve God, God shapes your life into something that will appropriately display His splendor.

Your life struggles become examples to you and to others of Christ's redeeming power, and your life story lends credence to the resurrection. In time, God makes you into a witness and provides in you a testimony.

The difficulties and hardships you face become invaluable necessities in the path of discipleship. They are all necessary if you will reflect His grace.

Do not waste one struggle. Embrace them all and offer them eagerly as good sacrifices to God – that is, offer in your heart even the trials as metaphorical burnt offerings. God gives a tremendous return for the ashes.

. . .

"This will result in your being witnesses to them."

Luke 21:13

YOU ARE FAMILY

The connection between yourself and God is deeper than you might think. It is more long-lasting than you may currently know. The connection is a blood tie. It is more than heart and more than mind. More than emotion.

God was the One who breathed His breath into your lungs. The life you live was His to give, and He gave it. And He would give it again for you today.

You are His family. You are His child. He looks on you warmly and with full intention to grant good things for your life.

You go to your Father to learn how to live. You go to your Father to gain understanding and instruction in what it means to be an heir with Christ.

. . .

Because you are His sons, God sent the Spirit of His Son into our hearts, the Spirit who calls out, 'Abba, Father.'

Galatians 4:6

HE CROSSES THE DISTANCE

In a still moment you may have a sense of God's drawing you near. A line that once separated your space from His is quietly moved, and instinctively you know He is the One who moved it. You know He is the One who took your face in His hands and closed the space between you.

This is what God does. He closes the gap. You may think you are reaching out to God, but ultimately you discover it was Him all along. He reaches out to you and you respond. What else can you do when the Creator of the world speaks your name?

The space between you and God is unnatural, and Christ is the remedy. In quiet moments you glimpse the reconciliation.

. . .

"Jesus said to her, 'Mary.' She turned toward Him and cried out in Aramaic, 'Rabboni!' (which means Teacher)."

John 20:16

HOPE UNSWERVING

You can live with complete confidence in the hope God placed in your heart. Whether you trusted Him first as a child, later as a teen, or even later as an adult, you can trust in the hope He gave. He is real and one day you will see all His promises come to fruition.

Do not lose your hope. Rather, build on the foundation of it. God is faithful, even if others are not. You cannot make the mistake of measuring God by the actions of the people you encounter. The created are not God and God is not created. Your hope will fail you if you try to understand perfect God by imperfect man. It must be the other way around.

. . .

Let us hold unswervingly to the hope we profess, for He who promised is faithful.

Hebrews 10:23

AWARE OF HIS PRESENCE

There is a relationship God alone makes available to your soul. Seek it. Ask for it. No one is like God, and communion with Him is preferable to all others.

God alone makes you aware of His presence. He opens spiritual eyes and spiritual ears. Pray He opens yours.

Pray He grants you the understanding that only He can give. Pray He grants you spiritual knowledge and faith. Pray for the wisdom that comes from God.

He offers Himself to you and is willing to lavish your heart with His perfect nearness.

God is the one good offered to you outside of Creation. Everything else He offers is from within the created world. But He is straight from Heaven. Pray He makes you aware.

. . .

When Jacob awoke from his sleep, he thought, 'Surely the LORD is in this place, and I was not aware of it.'

Genesis 28:16

THOROUGHLY EQUIPPED

Meditate on the Word of God. Allow it to become part of your mindset and part of your being. A single verse mulled over in your mind day in and day out begins to shape your thought processes and, eventually, your actions.

Add a new verse, when the first has taken root, and it too becomes part of your being. If you want God to do a work in you, to change you from the inside out, plant the seed of His Word and watch it grow.

God's Word will weed out of you what does not belong. A single verse is where you begin. God will reward the effort and your life, like so many before you, will be changed.

. . .

All Scripture is God-breathed
and is useful for teaching,
rebuking, correcting and training
in righteousness, so that the
servant of God may be thoroughly
equipped for every good work.

2 Timothy 3:16-17

WHEN YOU PERSEVERE

The end result of you is much too important to God for Him to cut corners; so do
not be dismayed by the struggle or when,
after much prayer, you find that all that
is left is to dig in your heels and persevere. Perseverance is a necessary part
of life's journey and a necessary part of
your learning to be the you God created
you to be.

God is revealed and experienced in a unique
way under the pressures of perseverance.

So learn to persevere. Learn to accept
seeming setbacks as experience gained and
par for the course. The current you is an
incomplete version. Perseverance is the
muscle work that brings about the perfection of your faith. Through perseverance
you are made complete.

. . .

Perseverance must finish its
work so that you may be mature and
complete, not lacking anything.

James 1:4

I will sing to
the LORD, for He has
been good to me.

Psalm 13:6

may

A HUMBLE HEART

If you think you have chosen God you need only ask, "Am I changed?" When your heart chooses God, you are humbled by Him, before Him, and before others.

God says that when you love Him, you choose His ways over your own. When you choose His ways you are humbled. You allow Him into your life and your life cannot help but reflect the choosing. It is reflected in your actions toward others and in your eager acceptance of all of God's commands.

God illustrated love and humility when His actions chose you. Can there be a more humbling example than Christ's blood on the cross?

Pray today that you might choose God and choose Him eagerly. Embrace the humility that comes from Him.

. . .

Humble yourselves, therefore,
under God's mighty hand, that He
may lift you up in due time.

1 Peter 5:6

HE DOES NOT FORGET

As much as you are crushed by life's sorrows, God is crushed more. He hears every cry and is witness to every injustice. God has not deserted mankind and every horror you witness is deeply personal to His heart. To turn from Him in misplaced anger is to turn from your only source of hope.

The anger you feel is nothing to God's and He has promised to set all things right. To repair what man has broken. To make Creation whole.

God does not forget the helpless.

When you are tempted to blame God for life's atrocities, acknowledge, instead, His place as Lord and Creator. Acknowledge Him as the only One able to set right a world turned upside down by sin.

. . .

Arise, LORD! Lift up Your hand,
O God. Do not forget the helpless.

Psalm 10:12

THAT YOU MAY UNDERSTAND

You trust that the Holy Spirit is in you. Christ promised the Spirit would come, and you trust that He has. And you experience daily His work in your life and on your mind.

The Spirit is what makes God's Word alive. He is the key that unlocks the thoughts of God. The Spirit helps you read Scripture and understand its spiritual significance.

Without the Spirit, or with an underdeveloped sense of Him, the Word of God may seem foolish to you. This is one more reason regular, quiet moments with God are so important.

Your relationship with God and your understanding of Him develops over time. Do not neglect it. When you read Scripture, pray that the Spirit of God will help you understand.

· · ·

We have not received the spirit of the world but the Spirit who is from God, that we may understand what God has freely given us.

1 Corinthians 2:12

BE THE CHEER!

Every face you pass in a day has a story behind it, and every story has a worry of its own.

And herein lies the great opportunity. A moment to lighten the burdens of a stranger or a friend. A smile as reminder that weary days pass and no one is alone.

Every person has days they need to be reminded of the joys in life. There are days of insecurity and days of heavy burdens. Days when you almost forget Jesus is by your side.

Today, remember to smile. Be the cheer that lifts someone's day. Remember the look on your face and the words from your mouth have the power of life, because there is Life in you!

. . .

A cheerful look brings joy to the heart,
and good news gives health to the bones.
Proverbs 15:30

THE REASON

The command God gave Jesus was a command that both directed Christ and acknowledged His authority, and the willful, obedient laying down of His life brought redemption to all. For this, you are told, God loves Him. God loves Jesus because He placed God and, consequently, humanity before Himself. Of course, Christ has always been greater than Creation, and when He willingly became nothing He at once reminded the world that He is all.

Consider this relationship between Father and Son. Consider the command that acknowledged an authority that yielded for the sake of love.

The One who is everything laid down His life for you.

. . .

"The reason my Father loves Me is that
I lay down my life – only to take it
up again. No one takes it from Me,
but I lay it down of My own accord.
I have authority to lay it down
and authority to take it up again.
This command I received from My Father."

John 10:17-18

LIGHT IN YOUR DARKNESS

When you are separated from God, you find you are spiritually formless and empty. Inside you, darkness veils a gaping space none but God can fill.

Yet in His love, God did not will that you should be forever separated from Him. And so He said, "Let there be light."

And there was. There came a Light brighter than any could have known. God sent a Savior. He would form you and fill your empty heart.

All of Scripture points to Christ. The Old Testament and the New remind you that Creation has always belonged to Him.

Read Scripture through the illuminating lens of Christ and see His story made clear. Every passage reveals His nature and His purpose and His meaning.

. . .

Now the earth was formless and empty, darkness was over the surface of the deep, and the Spirit of God was hovering over the waters. And God said, "Let there be light," and there was light.

Genesis 1:2-3

BE USEFUL TO GOD

You do not know what God has in store for your life. You do not know what opportunities will come or what challenges you will face. You do not know when God will say to your inquiring heart, "Not now," and when He will say, "Not ever."

And so you ask that He teach you to step when He says step and stop when He says stop. You go to Him daily and ask to be purged and refilled. You go to a Father who loves you more than any other and ask that He teach you to be His own.

You do not know what God has in store, whether today or tomorrow. Pray for preparedness and clarity of heart.

. . .

"In a large house there are articles not only of gold and silver, but also of wood and clay; some are for noble purposes and some for ignoble. Those who cleanse themselves from the latter, will be instruments for noble purposes, made holy, useful to the Master and prepared to do any good work."

2 Timothy 2:20-21

YES! FOR GOD

Your God is true to His Word. Always. And He has fulfilled every promise through His Son, Jesus. For this reason, you resound to God a joyful "Amen!"

And you pray that to Him your answer will always be, "Yes." That He would make you a child whose answer is yes to the work He provides and yes to knowing Him more. Yes to time spent meditating on His Word. Yes to seeing His face.

And yes a thousand times over to the dying of the self, that He might be known and that He might be all.

Pray you will awake every morning to God's voice, to His presence. And when you are invited to sit at His feet, pray you will say, always, "Yes."

. . .

For no matter how many promises God has made, they are 'Yes' in Christ. And so through Him the 'Amen' is spoken by us to the glory of God.

2 Corinthians 1:20

FOR HIS REDEEMED

There is great strength and guidance to be had in your relationship with God. Find a quiet place and take the time to know Him. Take the time to listen. Take the time to melt His Word into your heart that His presence might make you whole.

The mysteries of God were not meant to be mysteries at all. They were meant to be discovered and shared between your heart and His. They were meant to be talked about among believers and friends.

He is ready to guide you. He is ready to show you the way. His unfailing love, it is for always. It is for today. It is for His redeemed. And you, my friend, are redeemed. Live the life He gives.

• • •

In Your unfailing love You will lead the people You have redeemed. In Your strength You will guide them to Your holy dwelling.

Exodus 15:13

LOVE CHRIST MOST

What you pour into your life, what you hear and what you see, has a direct correlation to the person you become, how you treat others, and the decisions you make for yourself and for your family.

When you choose to believe Christ, you can choose also to fill your life with all He deems good and uplifting. The result is you are made better than before and more the person you were always intended to be.

If you want to offer the best you have to those you love, love Christ most of all. Whatever fills your cup overflows to affect everyone in your life. Let your life overflow, then, with Christ. The only way is to have more of Him every day.

. . .

So then, just as you received Christ
Jesus as Lord, continue to live in Him,
rooted and built up in Him, strengthened
in the faith as you were taught,
and overflowing with thankfulness.

Colossians 2:6-7

A STRONG TOWER

Go to God and praise Him. Worship Him. Know Him as Creator and as Lord. Know Him as a child knows her Father. You enter His presence as a child who enters the presence of a most perfect Dad, confident He is pleased to see you at His feet. And no one can touch the relationship you share. It is tender and deeply personal, unique.

Your relationship with God is unique. You can run to Him like you run to no other. You can trust your well-being is always His will. And the foundation of this relationship is the solid, unwavering love of a Father for His child. The promise is for strength and safety, and it is yours.

. . .

The name of the LORD is a strong tower;
the righteous run to it and are safe.

Proverbs 18:10

THE GIFT OF SCRIPTURE

God gave you Scripture that you might know Him more. That you might take the words and memorize them and melt them into your mind and into your conscience.

Do not neglect this gift. It is the means by which you can test the promptings in your heart to know whether they are pleasing to God. Scripture is the means by which God promises to renew you from the inside out.

To verbally choose God is good, but to choose Him by way of also choosing His Word is to choose to make Him an engaged and active part of your life. Why do you have Scripture if not to work it through? To expedite the purification of your mind and your soul?

. . .

Reflect on what I am saying, for the Lord will give you insight into all this.

2 Timothy 2:7

WAIT FOR THE LORD

Wait for the Lord. Do not give up. Keep steadfast in your faith that God is all and God is near. Keep steadfast in the promise that God upholds those who seek Him, those who long to see His face.

And you have longed to see His face. You have sought Him and cried out to Him. You have approached in joy and in frustration. And now, you wait for Him.

Because it is God for whom you wait, you are strong. You trust that you will not fail because God does fail; and He is working out the plan He has for you, even today. Even though He seems silent.

Wait for the Lord. Take heart. This quiet moment is part of His plan.

. . .

Wait for the LORD; be strong and take heart and wait for the LORD.

Psalm 27:14

NO ONE COMPARES

No one compares to God and there is no relationship like a relationship with Him.
There is no substitute for God in your
life. When you go to Him and His presence
is manifest, when your eyes and ears are
opened to His heart, how can you help but
ask for more? More of His presence? More
of the life He grants to your soul?

God is so great that only He can reveal Himself to your heart. You cannot grasp the
concept of Him without His help. Only God
makes you to see and understand. That is
why you kneel before Him and ask to stand
in awe.

Worship Him. Long for a God experience all
your own.

. . .

"To whom will you compare Me?
Or who is My equal?" says the Holy One.

Isaiah 40:25

WHEN YOU STRUGGLE

Make up your mind that you will sing to the Lord. Take Him your burdens, your questions, your concerns. Take Him your praise. Remind your heart that every struggle is useful for your benefit and His glory. No experience is wasted on God. No trial is too much for Him. He has a plan for your life, and even in the struggle He hears and sees.

One day this event will be a memory. Determine that when you look back you will know your trust was always in Him. When you see – and one day you will see – how He was always at work, determine to know, too, your eyes were steady on Him.

God has not left you. He hears every prayer.

. . .

I will sing to the LORD,
for He has been good to me.

Psalm 13:6

BUILD EACH OTHER UP

What is more important, to make a point or to point to Christ? And you point to Christ when you seek Him wholehearted and love your brothers and sisters along the way, when you lift others up and consider their needs as more important than your own.

You know humanity cannot become more or less guilty than it is today. Actions cannot justify. You know justification of Creation comes by Christ alone.

Therefore, lift others up. Help others to Christ. All are condemned without Him and all saved with Him. It is better to find Him imperfectly than not to find Him at all.

. . .

"Each of us should please our neighbor
for their good, to build them up."

Romans 15:2

CALLED TO HOPE

You are called to a great hope in Christ. This hope is yours regardless of what you have done, where you have been, or how you have failed. It is a hope established by Christ. Nothing can keep you from it except your own disbelief.

Do not believe a lie about yourself, or worse, a lie about your God, and miss the life of hope God offers. The hope is yours. And you can live it today. You can leave your past to Christ and walk forward.

Pray the eyes of your heart are enlightened. Pray for God to help you accept the hope He offers. Pray you might learn to live every day in Christ's perfect hope.

It is already yours.

. . .

I pray also that the eyes of
your heart may be enlightened in
order that you may know the hope
to which He has called you.

Ephesians 1:18

TREASURES IN HEAVEN

What captures your heart? What is the driving force in your life?

Your treasure is what moves you. It occupies your thoughts and is that on which you place your loftiest of goals. Ultimately, your treasure is where you look for fulfillment, security, acceptance. What you treasure is the place your heart finds to call home.

God wants to be your treasure. He wants to be your home. He wants to be the primary motivation in all your actions.

God wants to be your loftiest objective, because He knows He is the only treasure that will last. He is the perfect treasure. He is the only treasure that values you as much as He wants you to value Him.

. . .

"For where your treasure is,
there your heart will be also."
Matthew 6:21

GOD SEES

Do you find yourself in a struggle? It is easy to forget that God looks at the heart. God sees what is on the inside and pays little notice to outward success. God knows the ultimate victories and failures lie hidden deep inside the conscience.

Your struggles are not hidden from God. He knows the very root of them. He knows them better than you know them yourself.

And He opens a door for you that no one can shut. It is a door for those who know that Christ will overcome. Keep steady on your journey. Keep God at your front. He sees when you lack strength. He sees the struggle. He sees the hidden victories when you hold steady to His name.

. . .

"I know your deeds. See, I have placed
before you an open door that no
one can shut. I know that you have
little strength, yet you have kept
My word and have not denied My name."

Revelation 3:8

WHEN GOD SAYS STEP

Today, pray that God will make you a person who steps when He says step and stops when He says stop. Pray God makes you so attune to His presence and His Word you make decisions that are discerning and wise.

The journey God has for you may not be quite the journey you expect. The doors He open may not be the doors you are looking for. They may not be the doors you would choose.

Choose them anyway. When God opens a door of service, though it seem menial or unimpressive or just hard, walk through it anyway. You are a child of a King. The King. God. He is your Father. He knows the path and where you should go.

. . .

By day You led them with a pillar of cloud, and by night with a pillar of fire to give them light on the way they were to take.

Nehemiah 9:12

PURIFIED BY GOD

You are not sinking. You are being purified. You are not failing. Your spiritual vision is being made clear.

Even your noblest of pursuits is
tainted with vanity. God is bringing
you to a place where your heart's desire
corresponds with His and self-justifi-
cation is far from your motive.

Trust Him in trials. Remind yourself
daily that God is not your project nor
your creation. You are His. You do not
need to justify God. God justifies you.
God's work in you is not yet complete.
He is concerned with the final outcome
of you, with your purification. He is
less concerned with what others may
think they know about you.

God is making you His from the inside
to the outside.

. . .

He knows the way that I take;
when He has tested me,
I will come forth as gold.

Job 23:10

DO THE NEXT THING

It is easy to feel unfit to serve others. It is easy to feel that your efforts are small and insignificant. You do not always know when and who and how.

Do the next thing. Set your heart on Christ that you might be always willing and aware, and simply do the next thing. The simple opportunities to give of yourself may be opportunities that touch someone's life in a more meaningful way than you know. Surely the willing servant touches the heart of Christ. And it is for Christ that you give of yourself, because He gives Himself daily to you.

Christ, whose eyes see the individual. He wants you to see individuals, too. Individuals with needs and cares, so similar to your own.

. . .

Dear children, let us not love with words
or tongue but with actions and in truth.
1 John 3:18

THEY HID FROM GOD

God's definition of life is the light by which the realities of Creation are revealed. But the moment you hide yourself from God, you step out of His light and are lost.

Since God is the Light by which you see and exist, without Him you grope in darkness. Without the Light you do not know, truly, who you are and you do not know your place in Creation. You are left to be defined by something or someone other than God. A false reality.

God is the One who created you. God is the One who defines you. He knows why you exist. He is the only One who knows and the only One who can make clear the reality that is you.

. . .

Then the man and his wife heard the sound of the LORD God as He was walking in the garden in the cool of the day, and they hid from the LORD God among the trees of the garden.

Genesis 3:8

DECLARE HIS PRAISES!

In this busy, noisy world, find a pocket of quiet and declare the praises of God! Declare them in the morning. Declare them at night. Declare praise to God alone and in the company of others.

The essence of the God-with-us relationship begins with praise. When you praise God, you declare that He is wonderful and more than you would have known to hope for. When you praise God, you remind yourself that He is ultimate. You remind yourself that He is able.

When you praise God, you escort your heart and your mind into a place of peace and trust. And when you praise before you pray, you remind your heart of God's perfect ability to be your all in all.

. . .

You are a chosen people, a royal priesthood, a holy nation, a people belonging to God, that you may declare the praises of Him who called you out of darkness into His wonderful light.

1 Peter 2:9

THE LIFE CHRIST BRINGS

For all of the beauty in humanity, there is also a sickness and the constant threat of death.

The story of Lazarus illustrates the life Christ brings. The story illustrates salvation. Jesus promised that Lazarus's sickness would not end in death, and He promises the sickness in Creation will not end in death either.

This sickness will not end in death. Do not allow yourself to be overwhelmed by life's limited vision. Christ is about redemption. He is about renewal. And He is about the glory of God revealed.

For all of God's goodness, perhaps His children will know it more against the backdrop of this fallen state. When Creation is reborn you will know grace perfectly and as only God can unveil.

. . .

"When He heard this, Jesus said,
'This sickness will not end in death.
No, it is for God's glory so that
God's Son may be glorified through it.'"

John 11:4

A RELATIONAL GOD

To praise and pray and study God's Word is to put yourself in position to receive revelation from the Holy Spirit of God. His Spirit moves your thoughts and reveals to you truths about Christ and about life.

When you experience the "aha moments" in your relationship with God, the moments when your spiritual eyes are opened to some new-to-you reality, receive them as personal messages from God to you. Receive them as parts of an intimate conversation.

God is more than an inspirational thought or a story on a page. The relationship He offers is unique and quite real. And, like all relationships, it requires time. An exchanging of ideas and thoughts and emotions. The deliberate involvement of two separate selves.

. . .

Then he said: "The God of our fathers has chosen you to know His will and to see the Righteous One and to hear words from His mouth."

Acts 22:14

BE PATIENT

God is a patient Teacher. He bears with you in all things. He is consistent as He guides and brings you again and again to the Truth until your heart at last takes hold.

Often, you surrender to Him. You seek His ways. But then you continue in your own strength. You long to walk consistently with God. You long for a life where He is glorified, but you fumble. And God is patient. He is patient while you learn to draw from the Life He offers.

Be patient. Be constant before God. He teaches your heart. Know that others seek Him, too. And they seek Him as imperfectly as you seek Him yourself. So be patient. Be humble. Be kind.

. . .

> Be completely humble and gentle; be patient, bearing with one another in love.
>
> Ephesians 4:2

YOU ARE THE TEMPLE

The Old Testament temple was a building instructed by God and built by God's people.
His Spirit dwelt there.

Today, you are the temple. Christ made it
possible, and just as the Spirit once dwelt
in the temple building, today the Spirit
dwells within you. You are more than a visi-
tor; you are an actual part of the House
of God. And by God, you are being set in
place as part of a much larger whole. He
still oversees construction.

Today, consider that you are a breathing
stone in God's church. Ask God to take you
to the mountain, to the heights of spiri-
tuality, that you might know Him and understand clearly the realities of your unique
place as part of the temple of God.

. . .

"Go up into the mountains and bring
down timber and build the house,
so that I may take pleasure in it
and be honored," says the LORD.

Haggai 1:8

CONTINUE IN CHRIST

To come to the end of yourself and to live in the reality of Christ is natural for the spirit, but unnatural for the flesh. When your spirit surrenders to Christ, it gravitates toward Him. The flesh pulls against Him. The spirit wants God. The flesh wants itself.

But when the flesh is considered least important, the spirit comes to life. Where your spirit meets Christ is where you find a fullness of life unattainable without Him.

"Once I was blind, but now I see," is true. The flesh believes that it sees, but it is mistaken. Wisdom discerned from the flesh can only be a partial wisdom, because it is wisdom based on half truths. Christ makes spiritual eyes see.

Continue, then, in Christ.

• • •

So then, just as you received Christ
Jesus as Lord, continue to live in Him,
rooted and built up in Him, strengthened
in the faith as you were taught,
and overflowing with thankfulness.

Colossians 2:6-7

THE SAME AS CHRIST JESUS

Know Christ. Live by Him. And remember that His ways are not like your ways. His ideas are not like your ideas. His motives are not like your motives.

Not like your motives, that is, until your motives become the motives of Christ. The longer you sit in His presence, learn His words, the more you earnestly worship His face, the more you will see all of Creation as He sees it. The more you will live as Christ lives.

Be willing to change in action and in thought. Be eager to measure yourself against the probing life of Christ. Do, and you will come to know Him, and your life will be lived as one lived straight from the heart of God.

. . .

> Your attitude should be the
> same as that of Christ Jesus.
>
> Philippians 2:5

STEP OUT

Your confidence does not lie with yourself, but with the One whose path you walk. Regardless of circumstances, you can have confidence when you sincerely seek God.

Step out. God is capable to see you through. He is faithful. The assignment He gives will prove His capability. The assignment He gives to you and His help in its fulfillment will prove His dedication to your life.

Decide now to listen and walk God's path. His one-step-at-a-time guidance is for you and for today. God assigns each of His children to trust Him. It is an assignment that will grow you and stretch you and prove glorifying to Him.

Be brave in your relationship with God, eager to step out in trust.

. . .

My steps have held to Your paths;
my feet have not slipped.

Psalm 17:5

I will tell of the kindnesses
of the LORD, the deeds for
which He is to be praised.

Isaiah 63:7

He is before
all things,
and in Him
all things
hold together.

Colossians 1:17

june

THE LORD SEES

More important than where you find yourself in this life is how you get there.
Did you get there by faith and with a
heart deeply devoted to your God? Whatever the circumstance may seem to you,
did you arrive in this place as one
seeking the approval of God alone? You
are in a good place.

God sees your heart. He knows the motives
that drive you. He knows the fervor with
which you long for His face. When you
doubt whether you have heard God, cling
to Him all the more. God is forever in
control of your circumstances and your
eternity. Your life depends on Him. The
purpose of all you have experienced and
gone through will be clear in His time.

. . .

> The LORD does not look at the
> things people looks at. People
> look at the outward appearance,
> but the LORD looks at the heart.
>
> 1 Samuel 16:7

BEAUTIFUL FEET

Are your feet beautiful? Beautiful feet look for ways to live a life reflective of Christ's love. They know God's love is deeper than they can fathom. They pause and listen. God is with them.

Beautiful feet are eager to share with others, both materially and spiritually. They are eager to serve. And eager to forgive. Beautiful feet are not feet that look for the spotlight or seek approval or applause.

Beautiful feet walk alongside the glad as well as the broken. They jump for joy. They dance. They kneel. They carry the burdensome loads, often for the sake of those who cannot carry them for themselves.

More than the words from your mouth are your actions, are your feet. Make them beautiful for Jesus.

. . .

How beautiful on the mountains are
the feet of those who bring good news.

Isaiah 52:7

THIS IS PEACE

Seek God today. Talk to Him. Thank Him. Praise Him. Acknowledge that He sees you and that He is always present and always in control. Purposely remember God and rely on Him when days are easy and life is going your way.

In so doing, you develop a train of thought and a mindset that rushes to you in time of unexpected hardship. The peace that comes from knowing God is in control is a peace nurtured on the good day.

Then, when the trial comes, you are ready. Because you know God is ready. You are at peace, not because you know what will happen, but because you know that God knows. You know from experience He is able.

. . .

The peace of God, which transcends all understanding, will guard your hearts and your minds in Christ Jesus.

Philippians 4:7

TO FOLLOW CHRIST

To follow Christ is to let go of every pre-conceived notion. You go to Him. You sit before Him. You dig deep into the Word. And you allow God to define Himself and you allow God to define you, to define others. God's definitions are the ones to explore.

Cling to your own opinions and here the exploration ends. God cannot take you farther than you are wanting to go. If you wish to walk with Christ, you must walk His path by His way.

The way to follow Christ is one obedient step after another. Put into practice His thoughts. Put into practice the acts He commands. As you do, you will see His faithful, persistent hand at work in your life.

. . .

"Now that you know these things,
you will be blessed if you do them."

John 13:17

june 5

PURSUE THE HEART OF GOD

God wants to bless the work you find to
do. He wants to see you flourish in His
will. Pray for His guidance and blessing to be on you and on everything you
set your mind to. Pray your life will
bear good fruit.

Above all, pray you might know God more
because of and through life's activities. Whether in your career, in your
garden, or in the caring for your family, set yourself to see God in it.
Every activity you do can and should
be an activity in which you see God and
learn more about Him. Every activity
God grants you is an activity imagined
and created by Him.

Pursue life as a means of pursuing the
heart of God.

. . .

We pray this in order that you
may live a life worthy of the Lord
and may please Him in every way:
bearing fruit in every good work,
growing in the knowledge of God.

Colossians 1:10

WHEN YOU ARE HUMILIATED

When, in your efforts to follow Christ, you find yourself humiliated, stay the course. Continue to do good the best you know how. Continue your pursuit of God. The God journey you are on will come to completion, because God is always in control.

God is in control. So do not shy away, but seek to know Him, learn about Him, and walk with Him. Cling to Him. Always. Trust Him to direct your steps and correct your errors.

God is consistent and He promises to guide. He is persistent and always present. Any amount of humiliation you encounter, know He is with you and you are being refined. You are seeking God and He is bringing you near. This, too, is useful.

. . .

Those who suffer according to God's will should commit themselves to their faithful Creator and continue to do good.

1 Peter 4:19

GOD SEES YOU THROUGH

To love God sincerely and with all your heart is the one decision you can make that will never be wrong. Every other decision is made with limited knowledge. Every other decision may one day seem a mistake.

Yet God is faithful and His love flawless. He takes imperfect people who make imperfect decisions and brings them to victory on the other side. Every day He creates witnesses who can testify that He is good; His promise to make you whole is real.

Love God and He will prove Himself and make all things right. All people are faced with the dilemma of limited wisdom and understanding. But the God you love is omniscient. You can move forward with confidence so long as your heart reaches for Him.

. . .

We know that in all things
God works for the good of those
who love Him, who have been
called according to His purpose.

Romans 8:28

FORGIVE FOR GOOD

You are forgiven and you are commanded to forgive others; however, forgiveness is not easy. God did not say it was easy. Forgiveness was not easy for Christ. It cost His life. Now He asks you to accept that others are forgiven and accept that you are forgiven, too.

To forgive a deep hurt is to put yourself and others entirely in God's hands. When you forgive, you trust God's justice and His mercy.

Sin causes a ripple effect. Even though the sin itself may be forgiven, consequences remain. Others are affected. Each one must forgive.

You forgive because you belong to God, and the person who has hurt you belongs to Him, too. The forgiveness Christ offers is yours and for everyone.

· · ·

Bear with each other and forgive whatever grievances you may have against one another. Forgive as the Lord forgave you.

Colossians 3:13

GOD RENEWS

God loves you. He loves – you. His devotion to you is relentless. His plan for you is in full swing! It did not cease because you stumbled. He will not withhold Himself out of spite or disappointment. Rather, every day His story unfolds with the purpose of bringing you closer to Him, always to where you belong.

Praise God because He is merciful. Praise Him for His diligence. He is pleased to call you His. He is jubilant to see you made new.

You can trust that God wants good things for you. His intent is never to hide from you or punish you or weigh you down with guilt. To see Creation renewed is God's desire and will. What He offers.

. . .

God does not take away life;
instead, He devises ways so
that a banished person may
not remain estranged from Him.

2 Samuel 14:14

MOVE ON

Your God knows when to lift the cloud. He knows when to prompt you to move on. He knows where you should stay and He knows for how long.

Simply follow His lead. No need to be afraid when life sees change. No need to worry you will misunderstand or fall off course. God is prepared for your fumbles. Even then He sees you through. He teaches you how to hear Him. He corrects your course and shows you His perfect way.

So do not be afraid of letting go. Do not be afraid when one moment ends. Embrace the here and now, and when it is time for you to set out, set out. There is new life in store!

. . .

Whether the cloud stayed over the
tabernacle for two days or a month
or a year, the Israelites would
remain in camp and not set out;
but when it lifted, they would set out.

Numbers 9:22

june 11

KNOWING GOD

Christ is the sum of God's story. He does not seek to make Himself supreme above all. He is above all. And He is the key by which you know the heart of God.

To know Christ is to know God, and there is no other way besides Him. So do not neglect Him in your search for the Almighty.

If you long to see the face of God, to know His thoughts, to see His actions, then take the time to know Christ. Take the time to observe how He lived and what He said and when He said it and why. Take the time to consider why He is such a focus of contention and why He deserves your tender, unrelenting devotion.

· · ·

He is before all things, and in
Him all things hold together.

Colossians 1:17

GIVEN A TRUST

How important that you follow God because He is God! That you take His Word seriously because the Creator of the world chose to entrust it to you.

God was not required to reveal Himself to you. He could have made you and set your life in motion and left you blind to His existence. But He did not. God wrote Himself into your story and you into His. He entrusted you with the Truth that God exists and God is near.

The question, then, is what to do with this most important of facts. If you know God is real and He has given His Word that you might know Him more, how, then, will you live? What does faithful look like?

. . .

Now it is required that those who have been given a trust must prove faithful.

1 Corinthians 4:2

TRIALS YOU FACE

God is with you! He uses all things for your good and His glory. So do not be discouraged or surprised when you face trials in this life. Trials do not come because you are on trial, but because the Gospel of Christ is being made known and put through the furnace for you.

The ultimate center of every trial is God Himself; not that He wills negativity, but because His Kingdom is coming to pass. You live in a world that is becoming the glory of God.

God is the center. Creation is His. The trials are His. You are His. For this reason you can live encouraged! The trials you face will yield a greater return in Eternity than you presently know.

. . .

So that no one would be unsettled by these trials. You know quite well that we were destined for them.

1 Thessalonians 3:3

GOD DEFINES LOVE

God's love for you is defined by God alone.
He did not stop to ask how you would like
for Him to love you or how you would like
to love others. He did not ask your opinion about love. He illustrated its definition in the covenant and lived love in
the flesh through His Son.

The result of God's love for you was that
He gave His everything that you might have
everything, too. God's love is entirely
self-sacrificing.

God loves you not as a means of completing
Himself, but as a means of completing you.
By His love God brings you to life and makes
you more real than you are without Him.
God defines love and His love defines you.

. . .

This is love: not that we loved God,
but that He loved us and sent His Son
as an atoning sacrifice for our sins.

1 John 4:10

BE AN ENCOURAGER

You have an opportunity to be the greatest cheerleader in someone's life! To brighten a year by brightening someone's days. To remind someone they matter, that God is for them, and that you think they are great!

Very often the best gift you can give is the gift of confidence. A person otherwise confused and lost will rise to the occasion when someone in their life believes they can.

So cheer on! Ask God to help you see the potential He so consciously placed in the lives of others, and do not withhold your encouragement. Ask Him to make you a person who lifts others higher.

And as you encourage, imagine the cumulative impact to be had when God's children believe in each other.

. . .

Therefore encourage one
another and build each other up,
just as in fact you are doing.

1 Thessalonians 5:11

UNSHAKABLE JOY

A time is coming when no one will take away your joy. A perfect time. A time when all of God's promises will be realized. The promises will come to fruition and you will see, once and for all, the enormity of God's love for you.

Today you know God's promises in faith. In faith you accept what He says and you walk out your life; and as you step out you experience, one obedient step at a time, God's solid presence.

But one day God will say step and you will see clearly the truth of all He has said. The unanswered questions in your heart will be answered. You will know God fully. You will know unshakable joy. And it will last forever.

. . .

"So with you: Now is your time of grief,
but I will see you again and you will
rejoice, and no one will take away your joy."

John 16:22

GOD BE PRAISED

God loves you. He loves you and He covers you. He spends time with you. He makes you safe. He takes what was meant for your destruction and uses it for good.

This is the God you serve! He is not a God full of wrath and anger toward you. He is not waiting to see you fail. He is a God who has promised to take you under His wing and, when the time comes, to see you soar.

This God of yours, He has conquered even death for your sake. If He was mighty for death, how much mightier He will be for life!

For this reason, and for so many more, you sing, "Hallelujah!" You shout, "God be praised!"

. . .

Because Your love is better than
life, my lips will glorify You.

Psalm 63:3

GOD KNOWS HIS PLAN

When you struggle to know your place in life, remember you belong to God. Your days are His to direct.

Naturally, you make the best decisions you know how. You strive to learn and grow. But above all your place is to love God, to love people, and to trust He will direct.

You may desire to know the purpose for which you were born, or long for proof that God is pleased and you are moving forward. But even this you come to accept in faith as you trust God as Teacher and Lord.

You trust He has a good plan for you. Trust, too, He will accomplish it. Whether He allows you to know the plan is up to Him.

. . .

"I will instruct you and teach you
in the way you should go; I will
counsel you and watch over you."

Psalm 32:8

SELFLESS LOVE

The most productive place is the place
where your thoughts are not turned
always to the self. The place where you
are not concerned so much with your own
interests, but with the interests of
others.

When you are occupied with loving God
and loving others, God is free to do
whatever He chooses in your life. Self-
lessness becomes the most freeing gift
you can give to yourself. But when you
are the center focus, you limit God's
hand by the boundaries natural to
self-absorption. Selfishness binds and
blinds.

Selflessness, however, develops a habit
of being that is never outside of the
will of God. Its boundaries are always
expanding.

Put others first and leave your life to
the selfless will of God.

. . .

Be devoted to one another in brotherly
love. Honor one another above yourselves.

Romans 12:10

CAN GOD LIE?

God does not lie. Believe Him. Believe Him for the hope He promises. Believe Him for knowledge. For rest. For life eternal. Believe that Christ is Truth and what He offers is worth pursuing, worth having and sharing.

The first question after, "Do you believe God exists?" is, "Do you believe He tells the truth?" If you believe God is capable of lying, then you can go no further with the God of the Bible. If you believe, though, that His Word is Truth and He cannot lie, then you gain a deep well of love and promises that are trustworthy and meant for you.

Today, consider that God cannot lie. Consider your relationship with Him in this context. What truths are revealed?

. . .

God is not a man, that He should lie, nor a son of man, that He should change His mind. Does He speak and then not act? Does He promise and not fulfill?

Numbers 23:19

NO NEED TO WORRY!

Pray yourself out of anxiety and into God's peace. When you pray and when you worship, God is made front and center. He displaces anxiety as the focal point of your attentions. Worship unveils the glory of God and highlights Him as the One who has never failed, whose love is always perfect.

Anxiety is an ever increasing weight. It slows you down and makes you blind to God's presence. But it is a weight you do not have to carry or manage alone. Go to God, hourly if you must. He knows the worry. Go to Him. Praise Him. Be determined in your heart to worship yourself to freedom.

Pray for clarity and then praise God! Thank Him. Even this is in His hands.

. . .

"Therefore I tell you,
do not worry about your life."

Matthew 6:25

WHAT DID GOD SAY?

God's Word is not always easy to hear, but Eli wanted to hear the truth, and Samuel recalled to him everything the Lord had said.

When God's Word is a difficult word, embrace it anyway. Be willing to say, "Do not hide it from me." Remind yourself that God, Creator of all things, is speaking into your life, not because He has to, but because He chooses to. Because He loves you.

Embrace the difficult words of God. Honor Him with your attentive ear. Be eager to know His meaning, willing to accept what He says. Would you call Him Lord if His ways were no higher than your own?

And since you call Him Lord, treat Him as such. Apply what He says.

. . .

"What was it He said to you?" Eli asked. "Do not hide it from me. May God deal with you, be it ever so severely, if you hide from me anything He told you."

1 Samuel 3:17

PERSEVERING IN FAITH

You will receive what God has promised! He speaks into your life. He trains your faith. He gives you a good work to do. God teaches you how to put your hand to the plow and not look back. He teaches you how to persevere.

You have professed a faith in God and now it is important to see your faith through. It is important for you to persevere, because you have not yet seen all God will do.

You see glimpses of Him. You read His Word. You pray and praise. But not until your faith meets eternity will you look and see all God has done. Only then will you receive and know in full what He has promised.

. . .

You need to persevere so that when you have done the will of God, you will receive what He has promised.

Hebrews 10:36

HE WASHED FEET

Do you understand what Christ has done? Do you grasp that the story is real? Does the cost paid disturb you? There was a man who was God. He lived. He died. He lives again. And He says, "Do as I do."

Jesus washed dirty feet. He sank low into His own humiliation so that you would know God. He instructed the disciples to do the same for each other, because He wanted them to understand too.

Picture Christ on the floor at your feet. Jesus wants you to take the time to know what He did. He wants you to take the time to see Him humiliated and to let Him wash you clean. And He wants you to understand Him by the experience of doing as He does.

. . .

"When He had finished washing their feet,
He put on His clothes and returned to
His place. 'Do you understand what
I have done for you?' He asked them."

John 13:12

COMPLETE YOUR TASK

When the Lord – He is your Father! – is kind enough to grant you some work to do, do not waste time. Do not drag your feet or hinder the work, no matter how great or small it may seem. Instead, show Him what eager hands you have. Let God see you run to finish the work. Maybe He will smile on you and give you another task! You want the next task. So do not be too long in completing the first.

But when you compare the task you have been given with the tasks of others, you may find yourself discontent. Shake this off quickly. There is no place in you for such selfish thinking. It will only hold you back from God's gracious plan for you.

. . .

"Whoever can be trusted with very little can also be trusted with much, and whoever is dishonest with very little will also be dishonest with much."

Luke 16:10

HE SEES YOU THROUGH

Start to finish, God sees you through!

Through to what? Through a short term task? Through the growing of and provision for your family? To the perfecting of your faith?

Yes! God is the One perfect Guide for every endeavor you face. God is the One who takes otherwise menial circumstances and makes them to yield eternal reward. Don't you know He has more for you than merely getting through the day?

God connects events in your life and uses them together. Nothing goes to waste. He makes your days lean one on another, and collectively on Him. One day and one event at a time, God sees you through. He sees you through so that through every circumstance you might see Him.

. . .

Being confident of this, that He who began a good work in you will carry it on to completion until the day of Christ Jesus.

Philippians 1:6

DEVOTED TO PRAYER

When you pray, you make a conscious decision to walk alongside of God. Prayer acknowledges that God is an active part of your day and you are an active part of His.

The habit of daily, consistent prayer develops a habit of heart and mind that is left underdeveloped without this exchange between yourself and God. When you are aware of God, you are more likely to make decisions for yourself and for others with God in the lead.

In prayer you remember to watch for God throughout the day. You become more and more thankful for His presence.

Today, remember the importance of conscious, constant prayer. God is making you new. Prayer hastens the process. Prayer reminds you He is near.

. . .

Devote yourselves to prayer,
being watchful and thankful.

Colossians 4:2

TO WALK HUMBLY

God wants you to know the depth of His love for you and that His love for you is what makes you infinitely valuable. Equally true is that God wants you to realize your humble position before Him and, consequently, your humble position before others.

Humility is not self-loathing. It is not wallowing in regret, unwilling to release to Christ past shame. Humility is the maturity to see yourself honestly before God. Self-loathing says, "I wish I was more than I am. I wish my position was more impressive."

Humility reveres God and has no desire to see itself revered in His place. It knows it has no place near Him. Humility frees you to a pure experience with God.

. . .

He has showed you, O mortal, what is good.
And what does the LORD require of you?
To act justly and to love mercy and
to walk humbly with your God.

Micah 6:8

june 29

KEPT IN PEACE

When you are restless and your thoughts darting, take a moment to focus your attentions on the Spirit of God. Allow Him to bring clarity and focus to your day. God's Spirit offers peace to your soul. Embrace it. Claim it as your own.

This peace calms your mind and helps you to focus on the task at hand. So do not forget to stop before you start and breathe. Acknowledge that you are not alone.

Thank God for the day you are about to face. Recognize that He offers peace, and His peace is exactly what your busy mind needs. Ask Him for clarity, and thank Him that He is approachable, even for this. Right perspective from God brings right perspective to all else.

. . .

You will keep in perfect peace
him whose mind is steadfast,
because he trusts in You.

Isaiah 26:3

TRUST IN THE LORD

Pray you might come to a place of perfect trust in God's love. Fear causes you to hold back. Fear makes you to second guess, to hesitate, to argue with God and pester Him for your own way. But trust releases all tension. When you come to the place of complete trust in God's love and motive, you no longer fear your own vulnerability before Him. You no longer fight your need for His mercy or the truth of your own limitations. You no longer need to be in control.

No need to cling to self-reliance. Your insistence on freedom from God only chains you down. Trust God. Trust that His love is sincere. God will not abandon you. He will not see you fall.

. . .

Those who know Your name will trust in You, for You, LORD, have never forsaken those who seek You.

Psalm 9:10

How great
is God - beyond
our understanding!
The number of
His years is past
finding out.

Job 36:26

july

ONE VOICE

When was the last time you raised your
voice in praise? When was the last time
you worshiped God with others? The last
time you worshiped as with one voice?

Praise stirs the presence of God.
Worship touches His heart. You touch
His heart! You touch the heart of God
when you praise His name, when you lift
up your voice to sing, "He is good! His
love endures forever!"

Do not forget about this lovely privilege. Praise is a most holy gift to offer
God. Praise offers to God all your attention. It expects nothing in return, yet,
the return is great.

Fill your home with praise and your
home will be filled with God. He resides
where His name is revered.

. . .

The trumpeters and singers
joined in unison, as with one voice,
to give praise and thanks to the LORD.
... and sang: 'He is good; His love
endures forever.' Then the temple
of the LORD was filled with a cloud.

2 Chronicles 5:13

WHAT GOD SEES IN YOU

Do not be afraid to step out. Do not be afraid to try. God delights to stretch you. He makes you into the person He intends for you to be. And who and what He intends is more than you have dared imagine.

Yet Satan remains the great deceiver. He deceives you out of knowing God. He deceives you into excusing sin. He ensnares, and deceives you into thinking you are less than you are.

But you are a child of God. That does not change. God never changes. His plan for you remains the same. And the sooner you allow God to take the lead in your life, the sooner He will unveil what He sees when He sees your face.

. . .

My eyes are ever on the LORD, for only
He will release my feet from the snare.

Psalm 25:15

THESE WORDS

The Word of God should be as much a part of your day as the air you breathe. Would you allow someone else to breathe for you or take air from you? Yet too often God's Word is neglected by the very people who claim Him as their own.

Embrace Scripture as your lifeline. Claim it as your source for all wisdom, guidance, encouragement, strength. If God will mold you from the inside out, if He will set you free and guide you in the decisions you make, He will do it through the Word.

And who else will gift the wonder of Scripture to your family if not you? Who will be the ultimate example of the seriousness of His Word if not you?

. . .

> "Fix these words of mine in your hearts and minds; ... Teach them to your children, talking about them when you sit at home and when you walk along the road."
>
> Deuteronomy 11:18-19

NO SHAME

Do not be ashamed of your belief in Christ or embarrassed to pray God's Word over your life and over your family. Jesus was honest from the beginning that not everyone would believe. He was honest that the Messiah would be misunderstood and ridiculed. Are you now surprised? Do not allow persecutions to stifle your love for God. You have glimpsed what others have not yet, perhaps, known. Embrace God's Word that the eyes of your heart might be opened even more.

Embarrassment only hinders the spiritual fruit and blessings God has in store for your life. Who knows but that others will believe, too, when they see what God does with a life fully surrendered to Him. God is faithful! He will not let you down.

. . .

For God did not give us a spirit
of timidity, but a spirit of power,
of love and of self-discipline.
So do not be ashamed.

2 Timothy 1:7-8

FAITH AND OBEDIENCE

Obedience opens eyes. Obedience assists in spiritual understanding. You trust God by faith. You believe Him in faith. And by faith you step out in prayerful obedience, determined not to prefer one command over another.

When you fall into the trap of only obeying the commands which are exciting or daring, or which provide immediate results, or the ones that are easiest for your disposition or understanding, you fail in faith altogether. Faith and obedience go hand in hand. You experience one by embracing the other. One proves the other. One highlights the other.

You have put your faith in Christ. Do your best to obey Him in full accordance with His grace. Through faithful obedience you will see His promises come to pass.

. . .

"For I have chosen him, so that he will direct his children and his household after him to keep the way of the LORD by doing what is right and just, so that the LORD will bring about for Abraham what He has promised him."

Genesis 18:19

LET GOD IN

Lift your head to God! Make Him your ambition. Determine not to hide yourself, but to allow Him to purify every motive of your soul. Do not be afraid to pray, "Lord, I want to want only You."

And guard your heart against an interest in God that makes the relationship all about you. Guard against an interest solely concerned with what God will do for you and not with God Himself. He must not be a mere means for self-help or self-promotion. When the foremost focus of your relationship with God is you, you run the risk of abandoning Him when He does not play by your rules or when you discover His ambitions are quite different from your own.

. . .

Lift up your heads, O you gates;
be lifted up, you ancient doors,
that the King of glory may come in.

Psalm 24:7

CHILD OF GOD

Do you know that you are a child of God?
That His heart is for you and toward
you? From the beginning of all time He
knew your name, your smile, your story.
He knew what would make you laugh and
every circumstance that would make you
cry.

From the beginning, He made a way to insure you would not slip from His grasp.
Your eternity belongs to Him; love Him
and trust Him for your future and your
today. Seek Him out. Desire His ways before your own; be selfish only for God.

Set your sight on Him. Delve into His
Word as one determined to know Him more
tomorrow than you know Him today, more
today than yesterday. There is no higher
attainment than God.

. . .

You are all children of God
through faith in Christ Jesus.
Galatians 3:26

WISDOM AND KNOWLEDGE

Reverence for God leads to wisdom, because God, in His mercy, exposes your heart. He reveals to you the truth about yourself. Truths you cringe to learn. You had no idea.

This is the beginning of spiritual knowledge. This is the beginning of true understanding as you face, in honest, sin – the result of trusting selfish, misguided instruction above God's. A small sample of the consequence of pride.

God reveals your insufficiencies that you might understand the urgency for His perfect sufficiency in your life. If God is allowing you the sorrow of seeing your soul defeated, it is because He is offering sanctification. Thank Him for making you to see clearly! He does not leave you alone. He offers true wisdom, redemption, and life.

. . .

The fear of the LORD is the
beginning of knowledge.

Proverbs 1:7

ACTIVE FAITH

Faith necessitates action. A stationary faith is scarcely faith of any sort. It sits alone, stagnant, and threatens to dissolve into nothing.

But an active faith is a growing faith. A learning faith. To share your faith is to share yourself. You give for others the way Christ gives, daily, for you. The way Christ gives and because Christ gives. In so doing you come to a new appreciation for the blessings you have in Him. A new understanding of the mercies you are shown.

Share your faith in deed. Share in forgiveness, mercy, generosity, kindness, patience, encouragement. Faith expressed in generous, Christ – and consequently other – centered living is a faith that will know Christ more by way of showing Him. Of sharing Him.

. . .

I pray that you may be active in sharing your faith, so that you will have a full understanding of every good thing we have in Christ.

Philemon 1:6

BEYOND UNDERSTANDING

Who knows the heart of God? Do any know Him well? Learn to sit patiently before Him. Learn to wait for His presence, His voice.

The wonder of God is that when you inch near Him, He is more than you thought. When you seek to understand Him, He is more complex than you are able to comprehend. The depth and width of God's love is such that when you step toward it and experience its power, you also experience the overwhelming reality that God's love and wisdom is deeper and wider than you are able to grasp. God is too much for you.

Even so, pray that you might know Him well. Keep going. Move closer. Ask to see God's greatness.

. . .

How great is God – beyond our understanding! The number of His years is past finding out.

Job 36:26

A GOD-MAN

What a beautiful God! He knew His majesty was too much for Creation. God knew when he made the covenant to love that humanity would be unable to uphold its part of the promise. And so He became a little lower than the angels. He came to fulfill what His children could not.

God is too much for man; therefore, God became both God and man. He is too much for you, but you are not too much for Him. He understands both Himself and you, and He teaches you the Way.

You seek His will because God knows the way of perfect communion. He knows the perfect relationship between your heart and His. He knows how Creation works and how you work within it.

. . .

We see Jesus, who was made a little lower than the angels, now crowned with glory and honor because He suffered death, so that by the grace of God He might taste death for everyone.

Hebrews 2:9

LET GO OF FEAR

A disciple steps out. A follower of Christ swallows insecurities and lives God's Word.

You are not bold in faith because you look to the horror of your sin more than you focus on the perfect sanctification that comes from Christ. You stand, frozen and wide-eyed, mortified by the darkness of your own heart. Terrified you might fail.

But if you will take hold of Christ, you must let go of this paralyzing fear. This mistrust. Choose adamantly to believe Him. He promised to stand in the gap.

Seek Him boldly, without fear of your own weakness. You are weak, yes. You are sinful. You are incapable. Now step out. God is strong. Your weakness is of no consequence when you walk with Him.

. . .

The life I live in the body,
I live by faith in the Son of God,
who loved me and gave Himself for me.

Galatians 2:20

A DISCIPLE OF GOD

You are a disciple, now carry it through to the end. Do not begin and then fail to finish what you started. If you say you follow Christ, then follow Him. Step out with Him boldly and in confidence.

Your confidence is in Christ, not in yourself. You are confident that He is God and that God is good. You are confident that He is omniscient and that full understanding lies in Him. Be confident, too, that His instruction is worth heeding. Be confident that when God gave Scripture, He gave it fully aware of the times and of every generation that would come.

God is capable of instructing you. Finish the life with Him you started. He corrects every course gone astray.

. . .

"Anyone who does not carry his cross and follow Me cannot be My disciple."

Luke 14:27

HOW YOU BUILD

You have been given a solid foundation in Christ. And now, you build your house. You build your house in relationships, the way you respond to others – whether in love or in petty arguments and debate.

You build your house with the content that goes into your heart and your mind. Books. Music. Movies. All are shaping your thoughts, beliefs, and actions. All draw you nearer to Christ or steer you from Him. The influence does not cease because you are older now.

Be careful to continue to build on Christ. Guard the foundation of your soul. When your faith is tested, the building will stand or fall.

This house, this life, is in your trust. But it belongs to God. You are building what is His.

. . .

Each one should be
careful how he builds.

1 Corinthians 3:10

THE GIFT OF GOD'S PLAN

God spoke a message through Christ. He had a plan for Jesus. He instructed Jesus in what to say and how to say it. And He does the same in you.

To imitate Christ is to accept the plan God provides. To accept that God's plan involves His instructing you in what to say and how and when. He knows what life you should live.

God has a plan for you. It is a plan that is a gift and expects surrender. The plan is perfect and pleasing to God. And it requires you to die to your will and preferred way in exchange for His. God blesses and anoints the life lived wholeheartedly to Him. Pray you know how. Pray you never let go.

. . .

"For I did not speak of My own accord, but the Father who sent Me commanded Me what to say and how to say it."

John 12:49

GO ON

You will never reach the end of God. You will never discover His depth. However well you know Him, hear Him, see Him, whatever mercies He has shown, they are all shallow pools in the ocean that is God.

And yet He stirs you onward. He invites you in. There is always more about Himself that He is waiting to share. Always more of His Might He is prepared to offer.

God invites you in and He anchors your soul. If He did not anchor you, He would swallow you up. There is no fear in God. He protects, even from Himself.

Wade into the waters of God, persevere to know Him more. To know more of Him. More about Him. His wonders are endless.

. . .

Therefore let us leave the
elementary teachings about
Christ and go on to maturity.

Hebrews 6:1

LIFT UP YOUR SOUL

Your God, He will show you the way. No need to parade your worries desperately before Him. No need to fling anxieties His way. Rather, petition God as a child who petitions her Father, as a child who knows she is heard and He is able.

Lay your burdens at His feet and leave them. Then, praise His name. God knows what you need before you ask; therefore, gift Him a heart that chooses to rest. Gift God a heart that knows He is in control.

His love is unfailing and He will show you the way. So spread your hands to the One who loves you most and praise Him as though your prayers are already answered. Praise Him as one who is already free.

. . .

Let the morning bring me word of
Your unfailing love, for I have put my
trust in You. Show me the way I should
go, for to You I lift up my soul.

Psalm 143:8

HE COVERS THE OFFENDER

You have hurt God, and it is not okay. But His love covers you. He could have chosen to hold no malice in His own heart and yet leave humanity to the consequence of sin. But He didn't. Instead, He held no malice and He granted unreserved love. Now He is restoring all things.

Bitterness and anger corrupt, but God is not corrupt nor is He corruptible. Therefore, bitterness has no place in Him. Allow it no place, either, in you.

Follow the lead of God. He shows compassion. Forgive and go farther still. When it is in your power to do so, cover the offender. God covers you because you fell and He was in position to do something about it.

. . .

"Love your enemies and pray for those who persecute you, that you may be children of your Father in heaven. He causes His sun to rise on the evil and the good, and sends rain on the righteous and the unrighteous."

Matthew 5:44-45

GIVE GOD YOUR PAIN

God will melt the anger in your heart, the hurts, the wounds. He will heal every sore spot in your life. But you must take the anger to Him. You must leave all to His judgment and choose the salve of His presence over the resentment in your heart.

Do not ignore the pain. Do not deny you are disappointed. Do not withhold tears. And do not coddle the anger. Do not nurse it. Lay wrongs done you out before God and speak every word of life and repentance and thanksgiving over them you can find. Insist on choosing Him.

And when, throughout the day, you find you are returning to these angry thoughts, take them again to your Lord. His love will free you.

. . .

"The thief comes only to steal and kill and destroy; I have come that they may have life, and have it to the full."

John 10:10

PRAYER AND WORSHIP

Worship is attention and adoration turned to God. Worship sets aside all else in order to acknowledge there is no one greater than He. To worship is to stand amazed before God, amazed at His goodness, humbled by His glory, His mercies. Worship acknowledges that God is in control.

When your prayer times are absorbed in introspection, you are thinking more of yourself than of God. Take the time to meditate on who God is and allow your heart to be ushered into worship. Then, allow worship, rather than panic or fear or ambitions, to usher you into prayer.

Prayer should be full of God's presence. Worship reminds the heart that to approach God is a fantastic privilege and a most serious, holy matter.

. . .

There is no one holy like the LORD;
there is no one besides You;
there is no Rock like our God.

1 Samuel 2:2

WHEN YOU WEEP

Do you weep before God? The struggles in life are real. They are often excruciatingly painful, crushing. Jesus did not say He would spare you pain. No person is spared. Everyone struggles. What, then, will you do with the struggles you face?

God can handle your pain. Struggle before Him. Weep before Him. There is not one part of your life that should be dealt with apart from God. He knows all of you. Why, then, do you approach Him with such reserve?

It is a sickness to withhold yourself from God. When you pour out to Him, pore over Him as well. Embrace all He has told you, all His Word shares. You can be bold and you can be weak before God.

. . .

"Even now," declares the LORD,
"return to Me with all your heart,
with fasting and weeping and mourning."

Joel 2:12

THE WORD OF GOD

Read Scripture and expect to find God there. Search the Word of God as someone who unveils a delicate treasure. Take the time necessary to absorb the passages, to wrestle with any part of yourself reluctant to accept Truth.

Read the Bible. Read it well from beginning to end. These words are meant to be meditated on and worked over by your heart. Deep intimacy with God lies here, so do not be hesitant to pray your way through.

There are no quick answers and no shortcuts to seeking God. The heart that wants to find Him will find Him. This heart, in fact, has already been found. Now it is time to move forward with God. It is time to dig deeper with your soul.

. . .

When you received the word of God,
you accepted it not as the word of men,
but as it actually is, the word of God,
which is at work in you who believe.

1 Thessalonians 2:13

PRAISE GOD – HE REDEEMS!

You have not known where you were going or how you would get there, but God has known from the beginning! God knows every moment of your life. Praise Him for never leaving you, for never giving you up.

Even when you chose to walk in darkness, God's eye never left you. His devotion never wavered. You are a joy to your Father and His heart, though He is God, He is always reaching for you.

Trust Him, now, as Navigator. Ask Him to show you how to live. Accept the way He provides as a gift and a means to a fulfilling and joyful life.

And do not fear your past. Recall it humbly before your merciful, compassionate, and perfect Redeemer. His love never fails.

. . .

Stand up and praise the
LORD your God, who is from
everlasting to everlasting.

Nehemiah 9:5

CHRIST INTERCEDES

Christ intercedes for you. He offers Himself as Mediator and restores you to God's
presence. And His intercession is forever.
Nothing can tear you from Christ once you
are His.

For this reason, you may approach God in
prayer and know your prayers are heard.
Christ is alive and He intercedes even
now. God hears the words you speak to Him,
so pray with a fervor that is humble and
sincere. Expect to experience God in your
life.

Accept that God is not disinterested, nor
is He silent or in the margin. God is fully
engaged. Accept, too, that His presence is
enormous, consuming. And you approach Him
as one who is quite small. By the mercy
of Christ you are escorted to His throne.

· · ·

Therefore He is able to save completely
those who come to God through Him, because
He always lives to intercede for them.

Hebrews 7:25

FIRST AMBITIONS

Careful you are not so distracted seeking God's call on your life that you miss God. The call God has for you is God Himself. Any work He allows you to do for His sake will be a work that very often arises from circumstances you cannot know and cannot create.

Christ must be your first ambition. If He is not, your good works are not unto Him and are quite possibly unto you.

The call of God on your life will be fulfilled by His righteousness in you. So seek God. Love Him with all your heart. Love others. Allow His righteousness to develop itself in you and to overflow in everything you do.

Do this and God will take care of the call.

. . .

The fruit of righteousness will be peace;
the effect of righteousness will be
quietness and confidence forever.
Isaiah 32:17

FAITH MOVES YOU

Faith means believing that God exists. And if you believe God exists, your life necessarily reflects this belief. A step in faith is a step that truly believes God is in control. Your life proves your faith and your faith determines your life.

You believe in God. Allow this belief to shape your life. Allow faith to move you, to drive your confidence and your desires. More important than the choices you make is the faith in which you make those choices.

Actions are telling. You say you believe in God. How, then, will you live? How will the belief shape your life? And if your faith in God does not determine the choices you make, what, then, can you make of your faith?

. . .

Without faith it is impossible to please God, because anyone who comes to Him must believe that He exists and that He rewards those who earnestly seek Him.

Hebrews 11:6

FAVORED BY GOD

Grace saved Noah. God offered grace by way of the ark and Noah accepted God's grace in faith when he built the ark and escorted his family inside. Noah believed God and put his belief into action.

Put your belief into action. Accept the promises of God as true. You, too, have found favor with Him. The favor you have with God comes from the favor He bestows to Christ. And if God favored Noah, how much more does He favor Christ, His Son? And how much more will He favor you because of Christ?

You are favored by God. He loves you and He covers you with grace. Respond to Him with a faith that is deep and acts always in response to His love.

. . .

Noah found favor in
the eyes of the LORD.

Genesis 6:8

THE FREEDOM OF CHRIST

You were not meant to live apart from Christ. You were meant to follow Him and know Him. A life lived with Christ is a life set free!

Christ grants freedom to those who love Him, and He teaches them how to live out that freedom. Therefore, everything is permissible only so far as it is exercised within the context of Christ. Herein lies the test of whether an act is an act of God-granted freedom or rebellious sin.

The freedom Christ gives moves you ever nearer to God. It is a righteous freedom made righteous by Christ alone. Freedom that comes from Christ is selfless and is exercised with a discerning heart that is concerned with God and concerned with the well-being of others.

. . .

"Everything is permissible" – but not everything is beneficial. ... not everything is constructive. Nobody should seek his own good, but the good of others.

1 Corinthians 10:23-24

A HEART THAT COVERS

A heart that covers is a heart that has come to realize the grievous truths about sin. It is a heart that knows it, too, is sinful. This reality burdens the child of God, not because she is in bondage – Christ frees the sinner – but because she has seen and understood that Creation is broken because of the severed relationship between God and man. Because of offense.

And so the heart is merciful and it covers. The offense, the heart knows, is not something to be celebrated, mocked, or joked over. The offense is to be grieved, not paraded, the offender covered and given room to heal.

A heart that covers is a heart in love with God and a heart in love with humanity.

· · ·

He who covers over an offense
promotes love, but whoever repeats
the matter separates close friends.

Proverbs 17:9

ASK FOR WISDOM

There is wisdom for you only God can give.
And you will find it when you have asked,
and when God sees fit to open your eyes.
At times you will ask and the wisdom you
need will be granted in a moment. Other
times you will seek God for years. His
timing and lessons are perfect.

And when God opens your eyes to His wisdom,
you will know it is a gift from Him. You
will remember the years spent sifting His
Word and waiting for His voice. As the
wisdom of God unfolds before you and overwhelms your soul, you suddenly realize
that you know God. You trust Him. Now
thank Him for the special God experiences
that are all your own.

. . .

If any of you lacks wisdom, he should ask
God, who gives generously to all without
finding fault, and it will be given to him.

James 1:5

FIRST LOVE

Do you adore Jesus? It is easy to be swept up in God's work. It is easy to forget that work, no matter how good, is not God's work if it is not born out of adoration for Him.

And if it is not God's work, then it may hold temporal value, but it does not carry the power of the eternal. It is not lasting.

Only God anoints. The only way to live a life anointed by God is to have a heart in love with Jesus. Jesus accomplishes the work and, as the Teacher He is, allows the disciple to work beside Him.

Companionship with Jesus is necessary, because, in all you do, Jesus' presence is what makes life good and holy.

. . .

"Yet I hold this against you:
you have forsaken your first love."

Revelation 2:4

Who is He, this King of glory?
The LORD Almighty –
He is the King of Glory.

Psalm 24:10

May my prayer
be set before You
like incense;
may the lifting up of
my hands be like the
evening sacrifice.

Psalm 141:2

august

HE LIFTS YOU

God will not abandon His own, and you
are God's own. Your life is part of His,
your story a thread in His story. He
sees the pit you sink into and He lifts
you out. Only, do not struggle against
Him. Relax. Trust His direction. Trust
that He is in control. His ways are
good.

When you struggle against God, you are
insisting on self-reliance. But when
your eyes look to Jesus, He calls you
out, and only at the call is His strength
your own.

God's interest in your life is because
of His love for you and because of His
own compassion and goodness. Every
trial, somehow, traces back to Heaven.
Praise God He includes you in His plan!

. . .

He lifted me out of the slimy pit, out
of the mud and mire; He set my feet on a
rock and gave me a firm place to stand.

Psalm 40:2

FAITH THAT HEALS

The woman was healed because she believed.
She did not believe because she was healed.
Such is the authority of Christ. Such is
faith.

God asks, "Who believes?" and the ones who
believe are the ones enabled to experience
His hand in their lives. The ones who believe are the ones made to see His face
and hear His voice. They are the ones who
become witnesses to the great miracles and
mercies of God.

Choose belief and belief will choose you.
Belief allows the heart to melt before God.
It opens the way for God to work on your
behalf and for you to receive His blessings.

Faith reaps faith, but doubt steadily hardens the heart and takes away what little
faith you have.

. . .

"Jesus turned and saw her.
'Take heart, daughter,' He said,
'your faith has healed you.'
And the woman was healed
from that moment."

Matthew 9:22

TRUST GOD FOR TRUTH

The lie the serpent told Eve was subtle. It seemed harmless enough, but it led Eve to question God and His intent toward Creation, toward herself. She believed a lie about God and, in turn, believed a lie about Eve – that her best interest was not God's intent after all. And she chose to act on this limited perspective.

Lies about God lead to lies about you. Eve believed a lie about God's goodness, honesty, and sincerity. The result was she acted on a false belief in her own position before Him. She believed that, just maybe, God's way was flawed.

But God's commands are never flawed, His perspective never skewed. You can trust God's instruction, because you can trust God. You can trust His love.

. . .

Then the LORD God said to the woman, "What is this you have done?"

Genesis 3:13

HUMBLE YOURSELVES

The selfish life has not worked after all. And if it has not worked, something new must take its place. It is not good for believers to compete with one another. To be jealous of one another. To argue and gossip.

Christ offers a better way. A new way. A necessary way. And each must embrace it, fully. Each must be willing to humble herself before Christ. To kneel. To admit that Jesus is wise, that His ways are good.

To both accept Christ and resist Him is impossible if you will see your life renewed. Renewal takes obedience. Takes humility.

Humble yourself and Christ will lift you up. He will give you new thoughts and make your life to reflect the change.

. . .

Humble yourselves before the Lord,
and He will lift you up.

James 4:10

JESUS, YOUR STRENGTH

Regardless of your circumstance, you can rest, contented, knowing that every strength required, every ability you need, is found in Christ. And Christ is found in you.

You belong to Christ. He loves you with a deeper love than you can yet fathom. And in every circumstance, He is your strength and His strength is perfect. In every circumstance you can rest knowing that whatever needs to be done can be done because of the One on whose life you rely.

The strength you need is not your strength, but His. And He will not withhold it from you. Christ will finish the work. Rest in this knowledge. Breathe deep and trust that the perfect heart of Jesus, every day, is turned to you.

. . .

I know what it is to be in need,
and I know what it is to have plenty.
I have learned the secret of being
content ... I can do everything
through Him who gives me strength.

Philippians 4:12-13

LORD OF PEACE

Peace of mind comes in trusting what is Christ's to Christ, in knowing that what belongs to Jesus is more important to Him than it is to you. The outcome is His. The circumstance is His. You are His.

You belong to Christ. You are His to present to the Father. And as much as you value your life, He values it more. For this reason, you can rest and live in peace. You can live life to delight in Christ, in His presence. Your life belongs to Him.

Your future belongs to Him. He is the mediator by whom you have all contact with God. When you pray, He hears. He answers. He answers because you know He will. Your Jesus. Lord of peace.

. . .

Now may the Lord of peace Himself give you peace at all times and in every way. The Lord be with all of you.

2 Thessalonians 3:16

BE CONTENT

Allow your contentment to reside with Christ. Make Him the goal of your affections, of your life.

If Jesus is your goal, you will be content so long as you have Him, which is forever. If Jesus is what you pursue, then your life will be always available to Him. Christ will be able to direct wherever and however He pleases. The experiences to be had with Jesus are limitless.

But if temporal blessing is your motive for seeking Christ, then He is not the end reward. He becomes a means to an end, and your life becomes limited by your own greed and point of view.

You, Lord, are our greatest joy! To know You more, our motivation. Your presence, our highest goal.

. . .

Godliness with contentment
is great gain.

1 Timothy 6:6

THE WORDS YOU HEAR

Every hurt, every lie spoken into your life, must be taken to God. Do not dismiss harsh words. Only God can wipe them away.

One lie spoken to you, about you. Then another. You know in your head the words are not true. You think you dismiss them. But in truth, by not taking the offense to God you allow it, instead, to take root in your life.

Lies make you respond to life out of inse-curities you may not realize exist. They bind you and seek to define you. To dismiss an offense is not the same as taking it to God. If you notice it at all, it has the power to take root in your life.

God alone defines your soul.

. . .

Do not let any unwholesome talk come out of
your mouths, but only what is helpful for
building others up according to their needs,
that it may benefit those who listen.

Ephesians 4:29

OFFERINGS OF PRAYER

Still your heart. Quiet your mind. Turn your affections, every thought, to God. His favor is worth far more than the favor of man. His attentions toward you a precious joy for your soul.

Spread your arms wide and worship God! He is good and a smile on His lips lights up the world. A smile from God is enough to keep you for a lifetime.

There is no substitute for worship. No substitute for prayer, for God. Prayer is communion. A prayer of worship and praise is a prayer of offering. A prayer that pleases God.

Your soul thirsts for communion with God more than your mind comprehends. He is the life source. He is every good thing. With God your soul is complete.

. . .

O LORD, I call to You; come quickly to me. Hear my voice when I call to You. May my prayer be set before You like incense; may the lifting up of my hands be like the evening sacrifice.

Psalm 141:1-2

BUILD YOUR FAITH

Build your faith. Protect it. Trust the foundations set before you in Christ. You can trust that God's Word is true and faithful. Pray you are not led astray, but that your faith grows into a faith that builds the faith of others.

You have the ability to encourage others in the faith not because of yourself, but because of the One who loves you, the One who saves you and knows you.

You may at times feel limited in your understanding of God and His Word, but spiritual wisdom is not limited for those who trust Christ. God's ability to bring discernment to your heart has no boundaries.

So build your knowledge of Scripture. Take the time to listen, and God will fill your soul.

. . .

You, dear friends, build yourselves
up in your most holy faith
and pray in the Holy Spirit.

Jude 1:20

GOD IS OUR REFUGE

God is slow to anger. He is full of grace and compassion and mercy. And He is just. And He waits. He watches, unwilling that any should perish.

In the midst of complex God, in the midst of the renewing of all things, there is turmoil and difficulty, and often times your heart is very much afraid. Where is God when troubles arise?

The promise is that God is good and He is a refuge. God is your refuge. Look eagerly to Him and know He is always in control. God is aware of every eye on Him. He is aware of every heart that trusts in Him, that loves Him, that waits expectant for His return.

The future belongs to God. You belong to Him.

. . .

> The LORD is good, a refuge
> in times of trouble. He cares
> for those who trust in Him.
>
> Nahum 1:7

DO WHAT'S RIGHT

Sometimes right means showing kindness when you do not feel kind or patience when patience has run out. And sometimes right means diligence in the work God has set you to, however meaningful or meaningless the work may seem. Right may be the fastidious tending of the home and family God has provided. Right may be the job you dislike but need, or the relationship from which you would rather walk away.

God calls you to a life of spiritual fruit, and this fruit is manifest in a variety of ways. The work God has given you today may be preparing you for the work He will provide tomorrow. In any case, it is a work drawing you nearer to Him. Teaching you His love.

. . .

Never tire of doing what is right.
2 Thessalonians 3:13

QUIET MOMENTS

Quiet exchanges between God's heart and yours are often quite personal and not readily evident to the outside observer. The changes are subtle and within. Yet they are made evident in God's appointed time.

These private moments are moments when God is allowed to speak to your soul. Moments you listen especially close. Moments of praise and unspeakable gratitude. The attentive hand of God cannot help but foster deep spiritual roots.

Then, when the storms come, you are not moved. What has been hidden comes to light. Your faith proves firm. Perhaps you had no idea!

God's love is stored in you. And it overflows! It bears with others and brightens hearts. And all because of the so many secret moments you spent with Him.

. . .

Exalt the LORD our God and
worship at His holy mountain,
for the LORD our God is holy.

Psalm 99:9

SEEK HIS FACE

God is the One who moves you. He turns your heart toward His. He prompts you to seek the presence of your Lord Most High.

Do you see that the God who created all things wants a personal relationship with you? Do you see how He wants to direct your steps? To teach you how to live? The Lord places His hand on your life. He will protect you from yourself.

He will protect you from living in the unknown. When you walk with God, no need to fear that you are lost. You are never lost, because the Lord always knows where you are. He keeps you. He loves you. He knows you and teaches you about yourself, because He teaches you about Himself.

. . .

My heart says of You, 'Seek His face!'
Your face, LORD, I will seek.

Psalm 27:8

BEFORE YOU ASK

How marvelous to kneel before a Father who knows your every need. You can go to Him. You can bow in silence when you do not know what to say or what to ask. God will help you work it out.

In your kneeling, in your searching, your God, your Father who knows exactly what you need, will lay on your heart what to pray and how, in what way. He knows what you need. It is not for you to inform God, but to acknowledge Him. To acknowledge the necessity of His presence, the necessity of His hand and His will on your life.

This is why you go to Him, why you kneel and say, "Teach me, Father, how to pray."

. . .

"Your Father knows what you
need before you ask Him."

Matthew 6:8

THROUGH THE KNOWLEDGE

There is grace and there is peace for you. It comes in the growing knowledge of God, and it comes in the growing knowledge of Christ.

The well that is God is deeper than anyone knows or can fathom. However rich your faith, you have only just begun to understand Him. And so your faith is such that it continues to move deeper. It continues to build on itself. It continues to change and develop, so long as you continue in your faith. So long as you continue to develop the little knowledge of God you do have.

So do not neglect your time with Him. Do not neglect to seek God more, to pray, to put into practice the knowledge He grants for today.

. . .

Grace and peace be yours in
abundance through the knowledge
of God and of Jesus our Lord.

2 Peter 1:2

WHAT IF

Jesus said, "If anyone would come after me ... " If.

If you want to follow. If you want to know God, to know Him intimately. If you want to be a disciple, then this is how. This is what you must do. This is what must happen.

It is not a call to religious piousness. It is not a finger pointed to failures. It is not a demand. It is a statement. It is a choice. It is the truth.

If you want this intimacy with God, with Christ, then this is how it works. This is the only way it works. This is the way to experience what you have yet only heard of, what you have only entertained in your imagination. This is discipleship.

. . .

"Then He said to them all:
'If anyone would come after Me,
he must deny himself and take up
his cross daily and follow Me.'"

Luke 9:23

GOD KNOWS YOU

God knows you. He knows the you He created you to be. He sees where you have been. He knows how you got there. And when you have forgotten the identity of you, when you no longer recognize your own face or your own voice or the thoughts of your own mind, God is there, ready to remind you.

God always knows where to find you. He always remembers who you are. The real you. Not the counterfeit version Satan would have you believe, but the version of you He sees through the clarifying light of Christ. Through the healing and restorative power of Jesus. And He is eager to speak truth to your soul. He is eager to remind you who, and Whose, you are.

. . .

"For this is what the Sovereign LORD says:
'I Myself will search for My sheep and
look after them. As a shepherd looks
after his scattered flock when he is with
them, so will I look after My sheep.'"

Ezekiel 34:11-12

THE FUTURE YOU SOW

It is difficult to think how decisions made today affect the life you live and the person you will be tomorrow. One, five, twenty years from now your life will be, in many ways, the sum of the choices you make today.

But in a world where so much comes instant and prepackaged, patience and waiting are largely lost. Preparation is lost. Sowing and steadfastness are lost. It is difficult to tend the ground yourself when you may, instead, purchase the work of another's hand.

You do not know where God will take your life; but you will be blessed when you are conscious of the choices you make. When you patiently trust God for the results, both for the present and the future.

. . .

See how the farmer waits for the land to yield its valuable crop and how patient he is for the autumn and spring rains.

James 5:7

SEE HIM

The redemption you receive from Christ is a redemption and a salvation of the spirit, and it must be known in the spirit. It must be believed and experienced in spirit. Because God is teaching you to see with your spiritual eyes.

God is teaching you what is beyond the here and now. He opens spiritual eyes that you might come to understand and know the world beyond what you see today, beyond the physical.

Without spiritual training, you would, perhaps, never see Christ past His human form. But there is more to salvation than crucified Christ. There is risen Christ, and this is the Christ you know today.

This is the Christ you know in faith and will one day see, physically, in Glory.

. . .

Though you have not seen Him, you love Him;
and even though you do not see Him now,
you believe in Him and are filled with
an inexpressible and glorious joy.

1 Peter 1:8

HOW LONG?

Do not wait to accept what is yours, to live the life God has provided you to live. God has a plan for your life. He has blessings and good work and maturity of faith in store. But He will not force you to accept the blessing. He does not push His grace upon you.

Rather, He waits for you to open your arms, to reach out. To accept the inheritance He so graciously offers. It is yours and it is for today.

It is an inheritance of internal peace and unspeakable joy. This is the inheritance that makes your arms strong for your tasks, that makes you run and not grow weary. It is an inheritance that overflows and is God's alone to give.

. . .

So Joshua said to the Israelites:
"How long will you wait before
you begin to take possession of
the land that the LORD, the God
of your fathers, has given you?"

Joshua 18:3

THE GOOD YOU OUGHT TO DO

In the every day obediences, God is making you steadfast. He is making your faith stand firm. To do the right thing because it is the right thing develops a consistency of character that cannot be developed any other way.

Do you see the good set before you? The work you ought to do? God expects you to do it. He expects you to put your hand to the plow and to not look back, to trust Him for the details, the instruction, the outcome.

Do not put it off. Do not wait for inspiration, or the right feelings, or the right weather. Rather, be a person who is consistent, who can be counted on. A person who does the good she ought to do.

. . .

> Anyone, then, who knows the good he ought to do and doesn't do it, sins.
>
> James 4:17

TAKE TIME TO STOP

When you are tired and your list is long, stop. Set all aside for a moment to sit with your Lord. No one calms your heart like Jesus. Allow Him to bless you with His presence. Allow Him to remind you He is near.

And while your motivation is to simply spend a little time with your Lord, to enjoy His company and acknowledge His presence, you know that when once you have spent this time with Him, your spirit will rest. Your mind will relax.

Jesus helps you order your day. He always does. He reminds you what is first and what is last. He revives and sets the priorities. Jesus brings with Him peace and purpose and clarity of mind.

. . .

Surely You have granted him
eternal blessings and made him
glad with the joy of Your presence.

Psalm 21:6

LIGHT OF THE WORLD

Jesus speaks into your life and names you the light of the world. You. And He reminds you to let your light shine in order that others will praise God.

The praise of thanksgiving, the praise of a grateful heart, comes when fears are comforted, when needs are met, when hope is restored.

Jesus came as a servant and He grants you a servant's commission. Let your light shine that they may see God. Let your light shine that needs may be met. You are the light and the light that you are has nothing to do with you and everything to do with God and who He is and what purposes He wants fulfilled.

A light is a service to others. Provider. Comforter. Friend.

. . .

"In the same way, let your light shine before men, that they may see your good deeds and praise your Father in heaven."

Matthew 5:16

HE SEES

Have you seen the One who sees you? The One who loves you most? Who knows you best?

Today, reflect on the reality that God sees you. Every day. He knows you. He hears every word you speak. No part of your life has been a surprise to God. No moment kept from Him.

Ask that He make you always aware of His presence, of His hand at work in your life. In the lives around you. It does not matter where you are. God is with you. He already knows your future. He already has a plan.

Trust God's instruction. He knows fully the situation you are in and He will not abandon you or neglect to see this through. God sees you. See Him, too.

. . .

She gave this name to the LORD who spoke to her: "You are the God who sees me," for she said, "I have now seen the One who sees me."

Genesis 16:13

CHOOSE TRUST

To trust God is a choice you make. The joy, the hope that overflows, is manifest in you by the Spirit, and it is manifest because of this choice. Because you trust.

Trust does not always feel smart. Others may wonder at the way you so blindly follow God. But you know that you trust God because He is God and not because He has answered your questions.

Trust challenges endurance. You wonder, "How long shall I continue in this way?" But even this is a question to which only God knows the answer. And so you trust Him for it.

And the more you exercise trust, the more you discover joy and peace and hope truly do overflow. This is one way you experience God.

. . .

May the God of hope fill you with all
joy and peace as you trust in Him,
so that you may overflow with hope
by the power of the Holy Spirit.

Romans 15:13

THE LORD GIVES WISDOM

Your point of view is limited and you know this keenly. At times, the realization makes you feel inadequate. Overwhelmed. You may be unsure how to move forward when you are aware of shortcomings, of your limited understanding.

Praise God His understanding knows no limits! You can trust Him. You can move forward with Him. He will move you, show you the way.

Lord, thank You! You grant wisdom to our souls. You do not leave in darkness the heart that seeks Your face. You do not leave us to our limited understanding of ourselves or of You or the world around us. You are here, God. You are with us. We can walk in confidence because You are real and because You know all things.

Thank You!

. . .

For the LORD gives wisdom, and from His mouth come knowledge and understanding.

Proverbs 2:6

SHOW HOSPITALITY

One of the great beauties about Christ is the purpose He bestows to each person's life. The new creation, the new, born again life, is a life that ushers God's children into His very own family. As part of the family, each child receives a work to do. Each of God's children is gifted a special assignment in God's home.

He does not require perfection. The work is made perfect because of the One who gives it. He does not require full understanding. Again, the One who places you also teaches. God makes sure you know what you need to know.

And the work of each individual compliments the household. Compliments the Church. For this reason, each receives the others with joy and generous hospitality.

. . .

We ought therefore to show
hospitality to such people so that we
may work together for the truth.

3 John 1:8

RECEIVE GOD'S MERCY

There is a work God does in you that is accomplished by God alone. And because He is full of mercy, He accomplishes it. God makes His mercy come alive in you!

And so you move forward with God, regardless of how you feel. Regardless of what you desire, of what you think you do or do not know. The work in you is His to do.

Accept God is merciful and that He is doing the work. The effects of His mercies are not achieved by your own effort or desire, nor are they limited by what you lack.

Show up. That is all. Kneel before Him every day. Listen. Follow. Trust God to make the fruit of His mercies real for your life.

. . .

It does not, therefore, depend on human desire or effort, but on God's mercy.

Romans 9:16

HIS NAME

Because you bear His name, you may approach God and appeal to His mercy. You may approach Him as one who belongs to Him, as one who has been given permission to call on the King.

You do not call on God because you are good or because you are worthy. You call on Him because He is good. He is worthy. God is compassionate and full of mercy. He calls you His own. And when you drew away from Him, He took the necessary steps to draw you back.

You pray to God because You belong to His Kingdom. What happens to you matters to God. What you do matters to Him. Your today matters.

Lord, hear us. We are Yours.

. . .

O Lord, listen! O Lord, forgive!
O Lord, hear and act! For Your sake,
O my God, do not delay, because Your
city and Your people bear Your Name.

Daniel 9:19

GRACE AND PEACE

By faith you trust God. You trust that your life is in His hands, that He will bless the work you do, that He will guide and direct. You trust He is near, whether or not you sense His presence.

To walk in faith, not by sight, is a necessity. You are being refined. God reveals Himself as He sees fit and only as He sees fit, and every heart must learn the importance of the day to day living. Each must experience for herself that God is present in times of worship and God is present in the grocery aisle.

God is present. Therefore, the grace and peace of God are yours. They are yours in abundance if only you would live them by faith.

. . .

Grace and peace be
yours in abundance.

1 Peter 1:2

The mind controlled by the
Spirit is life and peace.

Romans 8:6

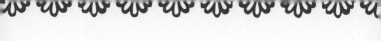

The darkness
is passing and
the true light
is already
shining.

1 John 2:8

september

BEAUTY TAKES TIME

God makes all things beautiful. Nothing stays the same. He takes the ugly, the broken, that dead weight of sin, and He rebirths it into a glorious reflection of grace. He makes mourning into gladness, into understanding and compassion. He restores the rejected heart and instills a deep well of love.

God is the Master of bestowing beauty to the unlovely. But it all takes time. It takes time because the beauty that comes from God is deep and lasting. Beauty is developed. Beauty is purchased at a great price.

Trust that God's time is good and right. Trust Him for the eternal beauty that is on its way and trust Him for the beauty that is to come in every aspect of today.

. . .

He has made everything beautiful in its time. He has also set eternity in the hearts of men; yet they cannot fathom what God has done from beginning to end.

Ecclesiastes 3:11

SHOW RESPECT

Righteous Christ gave Himself for unrighteous you – for unrighteous everyone. The cost of keeping the covenant, of keeping the relationship intact between God and man, cost Christ everything. His life. His Father. His throne.

Yet He was never bitter. He was always gentle. He showed respect. Christ always showed respect, and He shows respect today. He lives love and He lives respect. And He expects you to do the same.

Lord, help us to show respect, respect to those who are good to us and respect to those who are not. Sometimes this is difficult. We become impatient and incensed. Even so, make us to show respect, to treat people as treasures that belong to You, as treasures You have redeemed.

. . .

In your hearts set apart Christ as Lord. Always be prepared to give an answer to everyone who asks you to give the reason for the hope that you have. But do this with gentleness and respect.

1 Peter 3:15

SPEND TODAY WITH GOD

Today is new. Only God knows the words you will speak. Only God knows the deeds your hands will find to do. God knows every outcome of every encounter. He knows what yesterday will be tomorrow.

And this God who knows your future, He is near. He is not distant from you. He is so much more than a flippant evening prayer or a nice story to tell.

Lift up your day to God. Turn your heart to Him in prayer. Know that He is here, that you have direct contact with Him. Such intimate contact that His Spirit, even now, directs your day. The life of the One who knows your future resides inside of you.

Talk to Him. Listen. Trust Him with your day.

. . .

May our Lord Jesus Christ Himself
and God our Father, who loved us
and by His grace gave us eternal
encouragement and good hope,
encourage your hearts and strengthen
you in every good deed and word.

2 Thessalonians 2:16-17

LISTENING TO GOD

Listen. Hear the beat of your heart. The rhythm of today.

The Spirit of God whispers to your conscience. The more you practice listening, the more you hear. And the more you hear, the more of God your spiritual eyes see.

Noises around you threaten to overcome the Voice that matters most. But if you will know the sense behind that noise, you must learn to hear the quiet. To find the tiny voice within the still that speaks the mightiest and most important utterances of all.

When you do, there will come a day when you hear His voice more clearly than all the noise. The world will bellow, but you will not be confused. Because you hear the voice of Jesus.

. . .

"My sheep listen to My voice;
I know them, and they follow Me."

John 10:27

LIVE AT PEACE

As far as it depends on you, live at
peace. With everyone. There is a certain
amount of effort made for peace that most
would agree is good and advisable. But
for the Christ follower, the preference
for peace goes beyond the social norm.

The individual who follows Christ is
called by God to swallow pride and lay
feelings aside, to prefer peace and to
pursue it. There is no shortage of opportunity for you to humble yourself for
the sake of Christ.

And when you do, you walk in agreement
as to your place within the Body. You
agree to be the hands, the feet. You
surrender your will to His and trust
that what He has planned is good and
right and worthwhile.

. . .

If it is possible, as far as it depends
on you, live at peace with everyone.

Romans 12:18

A LIVING STONE

Every circumstance, whether joyful and easy or difficult and confusing, that God allows into your life is useful for the family of God, for fellow believers. God takes what you have been through and transforms it. He uses the moments of your life to refine you and to make you into a person you would not otherwise have been. He makes you a living stone.

You are a living stone, a benefit to those around you, and one among so many. So many living, breathing, moving, learning, growing stones. Each one supports the others. And each one depends on the Builder for its perfect and useful shape, and its perfect and useful place.

Trust God's hand as He works on your life. As He builds.

. . .

You also, like living stones, are being built into a spiritual house to be a holy priesthood, offering spiritual sacrifices acceptable to God through Jesus Christ.

1 Peter 2:5

WHAT GOD SAYS

Christ's will and instruction is at the forefront of discipleship. Not your will. Not your instruction. Not your opinion or philosophy. To highlight your own opinion removes focus from Christ. Rather, go as far as you know how with the will of God. Then, stop.

No need to fill the gaps of your knowledge about Him with speculation. Rather, respect Him with a holy reverence that refuses to place your own ideas in place of God's. Do, and your mindset is prepared to seek God with a clear and pure heart.

You do not want a counterfeit version of Him. You want God Himself. You want His words and His will and His teaching. His way is the only way that proves good and right.

. . .

I will listen to what
God the LORD will say.

Psalm 85:8

TO CHOOSE CHRIST

When you make up your mind to choose Christ,
to live for Him and through Him, you must
not be surprised when you find yourself a bit set apart. When you find you are
often left out or considered odd. Christ
in you means anyone offended by Christ
will be offended by you – and not by you,
but by Christ in you.

It will not matter what you do or say, or
what you do not do or do not say; because,
it is not you who offends. It is Christ.
It is you, however, they see, so walk always in love.

And you can trust God to use even this to
make Himself known to your heart and to
teach you how to live.

. . .

Yet for us there is but one God,
the Father, from whom all things came
and for whom we live; and there is but
one Lord, Jesus Christ, through whom all
things came and through whom we live.

1 Corinthians 8:6

THE SPIRIT IN YOU

There was a time when God's temple was a building, but today you are the temple and God's Spirit dwells in you. He could have chosen any place. He could have chosen no place at all. But God chose you. He chose each of His children.

You are the temple and God hears every prayer you pray. He sees you. He knows the words you speak and the thoughts you think. He knows the moments of your day.

Today, consider carefully that God dwells in you. Consider the intimate fellowship you are invited to share and experience, the closeness of His presence.

Lord, teach us to live in the reality that you are here, that Your Spirit truly does hear us, truly speaks into our lives.

. . .

May your eyes be open toward this temple day and night, this place of which You said You would put Your Name there. May You hear the prayer Your servant prays toward this place.

2 Chronicles 6:20

NOT AFRAID

You do not live in fear of what man can do, because man can do nothing that God does not see. No wrong will be left to stand. All will be righted. What is more, you live with Christ in view. You know time is nothing to God. Even now, in a sense, all things are made new. You wait to see the full fruition of what Christ has done, but even as you wait you trust it as true.

And so you turn the other cheek, not to make some moral point, but because your soul longs to live in the joyous fulfillment of Christ. In every way you are able, you live the promises today, whether they are now or to come.

. . .

The LORD is with me;
I will not be afraid.
What can mere mortals do to me?

Psalm 118:6

FOR THE GLORY OF JESUS

Whatever promises God has made, they are brought to fruition by God alone. And they are promises made for the sake of Christ. For the glory of Jesus.

Christ is glorified, and every bystander is overwhelmed, blessed by the glorification of Christ. Yet, somehow and in some way, the bystander often becomes the center. The bystander takes the place that rightfully belongs to Christ.

But here blessings cease for everyone. Christ is no longer glorified as the center of all things, and Creation no longer experiences the effects of glorified Christ when Christ is not center.

The promise, the blessing, may be yours, but you are not the one meant for glorification. Keep Christ as the center and you will be blessed by His glory.

. . .

In a loud voice they sang: "Worthy is the Lamb, who was slain, to receive power and wealth and wisdom and strength and honor and glory and praise!"

Revelation 5:12

CHRIST IS JUSTIFICATION

Pride longs to know victory. It wishes to be vindicated, justified in some public way. And yet you know public justification can have no place between Christ and His disciple. If you will follow Jesus, you must be willing to follow whether or not the following appears justified. Whether or not others see the purposes, the obedience, to which Christ calls you. Whether or not they cheer you on.

Discipleship is obedience because God is God. And the less vindicated, the less celebrated, your pride feels, the smaller your pride becomes.

Praise God for humiliation! When pride is less, Christ is more. When pride is smothered, closeness with Christ, dependance and trust in Him, is made stronger. The tie between you strengthens as pride dies.

. . .

I am not ashamed of the gospel, because it is the power of God for the salvation of everyone who believes: first for the Jew, then for the Gentile.

Romans 1:16

TAKE HEART

Everyone struggles. Struggle is part of being alive. Some periods in life are more difficult than others. Some lonelier or more frightening than the times before. Some more overwhelming. But one constant you can count on is God.

God is always with you and for you. His refuge is yours. His love unending.

God may not reveal His presence the way you hoped. He may not remove you from a situation or the situation from you. God's idea of healing may prove quite different than your own. But you can trust – always – that He is present. You can trust He is still the One who loves you more, and better, than any other is able. His love, His timing, His ways are perfect and trustworthy.

. . .

Be strong and take heart,
all you who hope in the LORD.

Psalm 31:24

GET STARTED

Are you eager for God to show you some work to do? Are you waiting for direction? Jesus told the disciples to open their eyes and see the work to be done.

There is more than enough work for the servant of Christ. What task is nearest? What need is in front of your eyes? One task will lead to another, so get started now. Do not wait for some deeply spiritual experience. Do not wait for a task that pleases your ego, or a task that seems exciting, or a task that will impress. Rather, do the work that needs doing.

Help. Give. Encourage. Establish. The less public, the less glamorous works are very often the ones most needed. So open your eyes.

. . .

"Open your eyes and look at the fields! They are ripe for harvest."

John 4:35

A TIME FOR QUIET

Worries come and blessings, too, and either can keep your heart distracted from God. Either can keep your mind just busy enough to miss the sweet presence of your Lord.

But your soul, it longs for the still, for the quiet place where your heart hears God best. In the busy hours of a blessed day, you may sense God's presence and yet find yourself unable to hear clearly His voice. In this moment you realize that excitement is good, but never in exchange for the One who granted the excitement in the first place.

Lord, still our hearts! Thank you for the life blessings you give. Grant us the discipline to find quiet, that we might share these moments, these happy times, with you.

. . .

Now, our God, we give You thanks,
and praise Your glorious name.

1 Chronicles 29:13

REMAIN WITH GOD

God does not ask you to change the world, but He does offer you a place in it. A work preordained for your hands where you will thrive, grow and come to know your Creator. A place where you participate with your Father as He changes the world, changes you.

This participation with God is a gift from His heart to yours. It is a life God alone makes good and holy and teaches you to live.

Molding the world is God's project. The world and everything in it belong to Him, including you. When the burden is heavy, remind yourself that the results belong to Him. Do not insist on carrying the burden alone. Your Father grants tasks that you might accomplish them together.

. . .

"I am the vine; you are the branches.
If you remain in Me and I you,
you will bear much fruit,
apart from Me you can do nothing."

John 15:5

CHOOSE PEACE

You know God. You trust Him. You have seen His attentive hand at work in your life. Now choose His peace. Choose peace daily because you have chosen Christ. You know He is with you. To wallow in worries is no way to live toward God of Creation. Will you allow yourself to accuse God of lying?

Peace is a state of mind and a state of heart. When it begins to slip away, slip to your knees. Do not wait. Do not put it off and allow anxiety to take root. Feelings will follow what your heart insists to choose.

And as you exercise peace you will have new, wonderful experiences in faith. You will see God anew with every choice of peace.

. . .

Let the peace of Christ rule in your hearts, since as members of one body you were called to peace. And be thankful.

Colossians 3:15

NO DECEIT

Unconfessed, unrecognized sin is full of deceit. And deceit is a true enemy to the child of God. Satan deceives you into believing all number of untruths. Untruths about yourself, about God, about people you encounter. This is one of the reasons God hates sin. God hates sin because He loves you, and sin is a lie in your soul. Sin counters every Truth God would instill within you.

Truth sets you free, but sin binds and blinds. Unrecognized and, consequently, unconfessed, sin keeps you from knowing, even, that there are Truths you simply do not know. This is the darkness from which God longs to set you free.

Father, make us to recognize sin in our lives. We run to confess it. We run to repent.

. . .

Blessed is the man whose sin
the LORD does not count against him
and in whose spirit is no deceit.

Psalm 32:2

NO OTHER

There is a spiritual battle between good and evil you must not ignore, and man is not caught casually in the crossfire as many would believe. Rather, man is the prize. Satan wants what belongs to God. And you belong to God.

But there need be no fear on your part, no confusion or concern, because the battle is won. You are bound by time, but God is not. He has already experienced your future.

All that God reveals to you, the instructions He gives, are all for the sake of the victory, the freedom He knows is yours. They are all for the sake of your belonging to God and your learning to live out that belonging, one faithful decision at a time.

. . .

Acknowledge and take to heart this day that the LORD is God in heaven above and on the earth below. There is no other.

Deuteronomy 4:39

HIS UNDERSTANDING

God sees you exactly as you are. He looks on all of Creation and knows what of it is right and good and what of it does not belong, what is counterfeit from the Fall. His understanding is perfect, complete. And His understanding of you knows no limit.

God knows how to reach you. He knows how to teach you His truths. He hears the meaning behind your every word, every action. When your heart was far from Him, God had a plan for your return.

One of the great wonders of God is the commitment He shows His created. His love is steadfast, in part, because He understands all things all at once. He comprehends beginning to end as if the future were today.

. . .

Great is our Lord and mighty in power;
His understanding has no limit.

Psalm 147:5

THE DEBT HE PAID

Christ paid the debt you could not pay. And now, you become a new creation with a new nature when you put off the things God never intended. This is how you cooperate with Christ. This is part of your choosing Him and acknowledging He has chosen you.

He did not die that you could continue to live in death, but that you might be delivered from it. He died that you could shed the death of self-centeredness and put on the life that is appropriately God-centered.

In His death, Christ demonstrated His love, and He demonstrated for you the love you must have for God in order to accept life yourself. And by His death you now experience all of life.

. . .

He was delivered over to death
for our sins and was raised to
life for our justification.

Romans 4:25

september 22

THE POWER OF APOLOGY

The question is not necessarily whether you are right; the principal of a thing need not be justification for an argument. Often the question is one of priority versus pride. Do you value the other person? Does your heart ache over discord?

Great lessons in humility require you to humble yourself for the sake of relation-ship, for the sake of unity. Is the quar-rel worth the cost of the relationship?

To bow before God, to choose His peace and way over feelings of frustration, anger, or hurt are necessary lessons. When you need to hear God's voice, when you need to hear Him remind your heart to choose others, to choose peace, over yourself, run to a quiet place. Breathe. Listen.

And then, apologize.

· · ·

Do not forsake wisdom, and she will protect you; love her, and she will watch over you.

Proverbs 4:6

THE GREATER CONTEXT

Hearts hurt during an argument. Tempers flare. Frustrations, opposing points of view, and differing starting points often cripple joint resolution. But however troubled you may be, there must come a time when you are adamant to choose God's way over yourself, whatever the cost. The outcome is not yours. Your feelings become inconsequential.

There is a spiritual context that encompasses all of life and every reaction to every disagreement must be viewed through the lens of this context.

The way you respond to others helps to move them and you closer or farther from God. So do not hesitate to take a time out in order to put God first. Do not hesitate to lay down your feelings for the sake of the greater context.

• • •

For in Christ Jesus neither circumcision
nor uncircumcision has any value.
The only thing that counts is faith
expressing itself through love.

Galatians 5:6

TRUE LIGHT

As you exercise faith and choose steady obedience with Christ, you see more of the Light that is at work around you. It can be a tedious task, but the more you live out the Truths of Christ in your own life, the more you experience and know His Light over darkness.

One day darkness will cease. Creation will no longer be torn between two paths, and the world will not be broken. Until then, you live in a distorted world on your way to salvation.

But when you exercise Light, your personal world will be more and more in cohesion with Christ. God will manifest, and you will know a stability amidst the turmoil.

The true Light is already shining. Practice living Light to see more.

. . .

The darkness is passing and the true light is already shining.

1 John 2:8

LIFE WITH GOD

It is possible to know of God and yet spend
a lifetime never experiencing the fruit
of life with God, of never experiencing
the perseverance, character, and hope
His suffering produces.

Do not suffer in vain. Everyone will suffer
in life, but some will reap great blessings while others reap pain and defeat.
The only difference is whether you walk
with God or without Him.

Pray you do not forfeit spiritual
fruit. Pray you do not miss the blessing
because you neglect to put in the time
to listen and apply God's Truths.

God experiences accumulate over time, so
make the deposits today and every day.
Take the time to hear Him. Take the time
to know Him. The relationship is deeply
personal and it changes everything.

. . .

We rejoice in the hope of the
glory of God. Not only so, but we
also rejoice in our sufferings,
because we know that suffering
produces perseverance; perseverance,
character; and character, hope.

Romans 5:2-4

THE TWO OF YOU

Jesus offers Himself to you as Lord, and also as friend, and as your Love. You want Him to look on you, bless you, speak into your life. Remember, also, the best relationships are between two.

All of Scripture, beginning to end, presents Christ. Grant Him your deepest affections. Seek Him as one smitten. Scripture is God-inspired for the glorious fact that God wanted you to know Him well.

You do not have to merely wonder about Jesus, you can pore over His Word and look on Him with great adoration. You can soak up His very existence. You can consider His life on Earth and learn from Him.

Look on Jesus. Find a quiet place and listen to His stirring in your soul.

. . .

"Here I am! I stand at the door
and knock. If anyone hears My
voice and opens the door, I will come
in and eat with him, and he with Me."

Revelation 3:20

PERSONAL CHRIST

The purist form of Christianity, of following Christ, begins in the private life. The inner self is where you choose Christ or reject Him. Behind the closed door, reckoning takes place.

If you want your outer life touched by the blessed hand of Christ, you must first welcome Him in the quiet, private moments of your day. Here you come to know Him personally. To know Christ deeply teaches you to recognize His blessings and all His blessings entail.

In private, He sifts your heart and lays your motives before you. Behind closed doors comes repentance and the acceptance of His gracious discipline.

To experience Christ in this intimate and personal way is the essence of Christianity. Alone is where you listen and He speaks.

• • •

Now devote your heart and soul
to seeking the LORD your God.

1 Chronicles 22:19

PUT ON LOVE

The person whose heart is full of anger and hate is a person held in bondage. This person is under spiritual attack from the enemy, whether or not they know it to be true.

And so, when you love them, when you seek out the prickly heart to show goodness, you are, in a sense, fighting for their soul. You stand on their behalf, ready to love because Christ loves you. And Christ loves them.

You love because you are part of the Body of Christ, called to be Jesus' hands and feet. And Jesus' hands and feet were pierced, so do not be surprised when loving as Christ loves proves an uneasy task.

You will be pierced, but love anyway. Because love conquers all.

. . .

Over all these virtues put
on love, which binds them all
together in perfect unity.

Colossians 3:14

GAZE ON JESUS

The moment your heart compares or competes with another, you are no longer in the will of God. You have stepped over a line and your usefulness to yourself and to those around you deflates.

A jealous person never lifts others up, but rather heaps heavy burdens on everyone around her. But when your eyes and heart are steady on Christ, you know the only One to be praised is God, and you know the only place for you is wherever He leads.

Look on your Lord and you will never want what another has, because you will want nothing but Jesus. He will keep you in His will and your gaze will direct the gaze of others until all attention is resting on Him.

· · ·

For where you have envy and selfish ambition, there you find disorder and every evil practice.

James 3:16

ALWAYS BE KIND

Are the words you speak kind? Is the advice you give kind? Are the thoughts you entertain in regards to others thoughts that reveal you to be a person of kindness?

Kindness is not necessarily a virtue in itself. Many people are kind. But for the Christian, kindness must be a kindness manifest from a love for Christ and a love for those Christ loves.

Kindness learned from Christ is not kind for politeness' sake. It is kind out of love. It is kind out of compassion. It is kind even when being kind proves belittling or humiliating.

The kindness Christ shows is a kindness that cost Him much. This is the kindness you are called to show others. True kindness, blessed kindness, costs.

. . .

Love is patient, love is kind.
1 Corinthians 13:4

For with You
is the fountain
of life;
in Your light
we see light.

Psalm 36:9

october

SINCERE REPENTANCE

Honest, sincere repentance is the single most important step you will take toward freedom. Repentance is the acknowledgement of pride. It is admitting that God's ways are best and submitting yourself to His discipline and instruction.

Too often God's children say they are forgiven without ever repenting of sin. The great loss here is that freedom cannot be granted without repentance. Repentance must be heartfelt. It is an owning of your sins, shortcomings, and choices that have landed you in the pit where you now sit.

And when you repent, then and only then will you know true grace. Then you will know a freedom that cannot be described, a freedom only experienced. It is a freedom unique to the Christ-disciple relationship.

. . .

Repent, then, and turn to God, so that your sins may be wiped out, that times of refreshing may come from the Lord.

Acts 3:19

JOYFUL SONGS

Today, give thanks! Sing praise! Shout for joy, and worship your God with gladness! You know God is good and you belong to Him. God made you and He watches over you and your family.

Approach Him with thanksgiving, because the God who made you loves you. The God who made you loves the ones you love! He watches over you. He sees the actions of every day and knows the workings of your heart.

Your God, this God who calls you His own, His view of you is an all-knowing view. When He looks on you, He sees to your very core. And He loves you.

God. Loves. You! His faithfulness is forever, and forever beyond understanding. Praise your God!

. . .

Worship the LORD with gladness;
come before Him with joyful songs.

Psalm 100:2

TRUST GOD'S PLAN

God knows every day of your life. He has a plan for you, and He knows the perfect time for every activity He has in store. Often you run ahead or look behind. You fret over past mistakes. God knows the person of your past, and He knew the person you would become. And He has a plan. It is a plan for your future and a plan for today.

When God planned your steps, He knew every choice, wise and unwise, you would make. But your mistakes were never too much for God. He knew the day your heart would turn to His. And knowing this day would come, God had a plan. A good plan for the day your heart would know His own.

. . .

There is a time for everything, and a season for every activity under heaven.

Ecclesiastes 3:1

WHEN YOU BELIEVE

The praise that comes from man is obtained by works, by intelligence, by wealth. It does not necessarily require any earnestness or true conviction on your part, only action found pleasing to society. But the praise that comes from God is received when you humble yourself before Him. When you look at His Word and accept what Scripture teaches about His Son.

This acceptance of Christ proves itself in the life choices you make. Because, when you believe Christ, and when you take this belief seriously, then you put His Words into action, because you are convinced of His presence and holiness.

And then, because your convictions are full of Truth, you are filled by God. You are changed by His love. You are transformed.

. . .

"How can you believe if you
accept praise from one another,
yet make no effort to obtain the
praise that comes from the only God?"

John 5:44

LOOK UP

Have you struggled to find approval and love from someone close to you? Leah was unloved by her husband. Jacob had eyes for Rachel. No matter what Leah did, no matter how many sons she gave him, she could not win the approval of this man.

"Maybe this time," she told herself. Every blessing God gave her she took to Jacob. But then she looked up. God gave another son, Judah, and instead of taking him to Jacob for approval, she took him to God.

God used Leah in ways she would never know. His plan for her was good, even though her heart ached. Rejection hurts. Even so, look up. God's plan and approval is so much larger than the here and now.

. . .

She conceived again, and when she gave birth to a son she said, "This time I will praise the LORD." So she named him Judah. Then she stopped having children.

Genesis 29:35

YOU BELONG TO THE LORD

Your life was meant to be lived with God and to God. You were created in such a way that you function at your very best when you are operating alongside of Christ. You were never meant to be separated from Him. You were never meant to go it alone.

When you experience turmoil because of choices that disagree with God, this turmoil is not a judgment as much as a consequence. And when you are blessed because of God's nearness, this blessing is not a pat on the back, but an effect of the glorious presence of God. God is mighty, and He both overwhelms and soothes.

Praise God He created you with a need only He can fill! Praise Him. Seek Him.

. . .

For none of us lives to himself alone
and none of us dies to himself alone.
If we live, we live to the Lord; and if
we die, we die to the Lord. So, whether
we live or die, we belong to the Lord.

Romans 14:7-8

MAKE WISE CHOICES

The choices you make for today are choices that shape your future and shape the future of those closest to you. You seek God's will. You desire wisdom. And yet, at times, the heart wants what the heart wants, regardless. You are in a struggle of the will.

This struggle, too, shapes you. It is important for your faith, for your relationship with Christ. Hold tight to God. Take the choice and your desire to Him again and again. Rebuke your own will if you must, but do not wait when a moment of clarity comes. When you know in your spirit what God prefers, rush to it.

But if you continue to entertain thoughts of your own will, He will grant you your way.

. . .

For with You is the fountain of life;
in Your light we see light.

Psalm 36:9

CHRISTIAN SPIRITUALITY

Take the time to still your heart, to still your mind. Wait for God.

God will speak into your life. He will direct you. But how will you hear Him if you do not learn to listen? How will you follow Him if you do not first learn to recognize His form?

God loves you. He will not leave you. You can count on this truth. To love you and stay with you are promises and actions made by God. They do not depend on you.

But many aspects to experiencing God and learning to be a disciple are yours to take or leave behind. Determine to experience all of God you are able! Find the quiet place. Cultivate a sensitivity to His presence.

. . .

"The Counselor, the Holy Spirit, whom the Father will send in My name, will teach you all things and will remind you of everything I have said to you."

John 14:26

THE TRINITY

If you are waiting to hear God, look to Christ. Every word Jesus speaks is a word from the Father.

From the moment Creation was separated from Him, God began moving ever nearer to those He loves. First, He spoke by prophets, dreams, and visions. Then, He spoke as God on Earth, as Christ, Messiah. Now, His Spirit resides in you. You have become a temple whereby you experience and know the Father, Son, and Spirit.

Study the Words of Christ. His Words are the Words of God. His life, your Father incarnate. And His Words are the words that stir the Holy Spirit within. Know Christ and you know the full Trinity!

And when you know the Trinity, you recognize His voice, His Truth.

. . .

But in these last days He has spoken to us by His Son, whom He appointed heir of all things, and through whom He made the universe.

Hebrews 1:2

THE WORD OF CHRIST

The life of Christ makes the Word of God complete. Christ brings to fruition all of Scripture and makes true every promise God has revealed. What is more, the message of Christ molds your personal faith and gives instruction for the path of your life. If you want faith, knowledge, and understanding of God, then know, fully, the message of Christ.

The Christian belief is that God is real and that history points to Christ as the Son of God. Praise Him! Thank Him, because His life was recorded and known. He knew what words would be written. He knew you would read them today.

God's knowledge is infinite. His love perfect and always prepared. The message of Christ, of God, was written for you.

. . .

Consequently, faith comes from hearing the message, and the message is heard through the word of Christ.

Romans 10:17

TO OTHERS

The command is simple. Do to others as you would have them do to you. Turn the table. Consider yourself in their place. This is what Christ expects from every Christian, and it does not matter if the person is your friend, a stranger, someone who has been good to you, or an enemy. Do to others as you would have them do to you.

It is an action easier said than done, and an action that clears the way for Christ to be seen and known. A small act with potential for everlasting consequences. An act to place Christ in the forefront and an act whereby you refuse to be the reason another heart stumbles.

Make your love for Christ the motive behind every action.

. . .

> "Do to others as you would
> have them do to you."
>
> Luke 6:31

A NEW CREATION

As you learn to walk with God, to trust Him and walk in His light, there must come a time whereby you let go of past regrets and ways in order to live in God's today. Christ promises to make you a new creation.

You! A new creation. A new self full of new hopes, new dreams, and new opportunities. It is a new you with a new mindset, a new way of making decisions and dealing with uncertainty.

But when you hold on to the past, you begin to forfeit the beautiful future God has for your life. Your past is no challenge to God, but He will not force you to let it go. The only one clinging to regret is you.

· · ·

Therefore, if anyone is in Christ,
he is a new creation;
the old has gone, the new has come!

2 Corinthians 5:17

LET GOD MAKE YOU

Trust God to direct your steps. Trust Him to make the way, to protect you physically, emotionally. Trust Him with your reputation.

When a malicious heart comes against you, it is difficult not to defend yourself. Even so, leave your reputation and its justification to God.

God knows what is truly important in the whole of eternity. And He knows what is not. And He is teaching you how to see the bigger picture. God is teaching you to see the eternal, spiritual context in which you live.

Consider the larger context and your heart, your emotions, will be less inclined toward petty arguments. Quiet your heart, still your frustrations, and let God be God in your life. Let Him make your way, make you.

· · ·

Be still before the LORD and wait patiently for Him; do not fret when men succeed in their ways, when they carry out their wicked schemes.

Psalm 37:7

GOD IS FOR YOU!

An anxious heart is a heart that carries and dwells on the burdensome worries of the unknown. These worries are not yours to carry, so why allow your heart such trouble? Why nurture a faith that flounders? Anxiety focuses on tomorrow today. But what you are given is today. The time you have is now.

Do not allow anxiety about tomorrow to shut you down today. Rather, walk in wisdom for the present and trust God for every second of your future.

The anxiety you carry moves you to respond to life in fear. Respond, instead, with confidence in the wonderful provision and faithfulness of God! When you do, you put off anxiety in favor of God's provision and build a faith prepared for every trial.

. . .

My God will meet all your
needs according to His glorious
riches in Christ Jesus.

Philippians 4:19

TRUST. DWELL. ENJOY!

Trust. Do good. Dwell. Enjoy. What a refreshing reminder! What burdens these words lift from the heavy heart!

You cannot control the actions of others. If others choose bitterness, if they choose malice, if they choose to do more harm than good, there is often little you can do. But God never burdened you with the instruction to convict another's heart.

Rather, trust God. Do good where you are able. Dwell where God places you today, and enjoy the sanctuary of your Savior. God will take care of the rest. The bitter heart is God's to convict, to heal. And while it is important to show love, to lift them in prayer to God, the burden of their actions does not lie with you.

. . .

Trust in the LORD and do good; dwell in the land and enjoy safe pasture.

Psalm 37:3

TEACH US TO LOVE

God calls each of His children into love. By His own love for you, He calls you to love others. And the love God requires of you is demonstrated through Christ. Look to Christ and you learn how to love. The love Christ presents is sacrificial and pure.

Christ gave His life. He meets needs. He heals. The love of Christ is a love that is selfless.

Often love is misrepresented solely as affirmation. But the love Christ gives is so much more! It moves you to give of yourself for the sake of others.

Father, teach us to love. Help us to see clearly every way in which you have loved us, and reveal to us how to offer this same love to others.

. . .

We know and rely on the love God has
for us. God is love. Whoever lives
in love lives in God, and God in him.

1 John 4:16

EVERYTHING IN CHRIST

You have everything you need in Christ.
Everything. Everything for life. Everything for service to others. Every provision is yours. Pray Christ makes you
aware. Pray He teaches you how to cultivate this most amazing of gifts.

The life Christ offers is not limited for
a select few. The life He offers is for
everyone. For you. The invitation to
worship, to know God, to recognize His
Spirit, is an invitation for which every
believer is fully equipped to accept.

When you know Christ, when His Spirit
abides in you, you are equipped to know
Him as personally as any person of your
generation is able to know Him. God does
not choose one believer over another. His
love, His presence, is yours. Wholly.

. . .

His divine power has given us everything
we need for life and godliness
through our knowledge of Him who called
us by His own glory and goodness.

2 Peter 1:3

HE IS WITH YOU

Your God, He goes before you. He knows your past. He knows your future. He knows every obstacle you face. He knows the obstacles within you and the obstacles without. And He says, "Do not be afraid; do not be discouraged."

You can walk forward because you know God is with you. When your life is His — because your life is His — every step you take belongs to Him. He will never leave you. He will never ask you to go it alone.

When you are trusting God, you can make the choice to obey Him and leave every outcome to His will. You are responsible for how much you love God, how much you follow after Him. And He is responsible for you.

. . .

"The LORD Himself goes before you and will be with you; He will never leave you nor forsake you. Do not be afraid; do not be discouraged."

Deuteronomy 31:8

SEEK COUNSEL

When was the last time you sought counsel? When was the last time you took
advice from a friend? The godly people
in your life want to see you succeed.
They want good things for you. And they
are part of the family of God, just as
you are a part! So do not hesitate to
seek their advice. And do not resist
advice offered from a God honoring
friend.

Often, others can see a circumstance
better than you. They are on the outside
looking in. You may struggle to see
what is quite obvious to another, so
listen to their words. Listen and do not
allow pride to keep you from wise life
choices. Choices to lift you up and move
you forward.

. . .

Listen to advice and accept instruction,
and in the end you will be wise.

Proverbs 19:20

GOOD MORNING

When you take a few moments at the start of the day to sit quietly before God, to still your soul, to listen for the Spirit, everything changes. Everything changes when you start the day in acknowledgment of your need of Christ for every activity.

Remember, then, to pray. Remember how. Remember to take a moment, every day, to sit with God. To listen for His Spirit. To still your soul.

It is good to study God's Word. It is good to listen to sermons or read how to apply Christ's teaching to your life. But nothing takes the place of sitting before Him. Nothing takes the place of acknowledging to God the necessity of Him.

Nothing takes the place of God. Of quiet prayer.

. . .

Satisfy us in the morning with Your
unfailing love, that we may sing for
joy and be glad all our days.

Psalm 90:14

ALL THINGS

If God is able to create the world and redeem every soul, surely nothing is too much for Him. All things are possible for God. And this God who can do all things, is a God who loves you and has made a way in His Son for you to know Him, hear Him, and experience His hand at work in your life.

This is the God you serve. He wants to reveal Himself to you. He would not instruct you to pray to Him, to ask of Him, if He did not intend to respond. So you can go to God with confidence.

Go to Him with confidence and go to Him with humility. Humility, because you approach Almighty God. He already hears you.

. . .

"Jesus looked at them and said,
'With man this is impossible, but
with God all things are possible.'"

Matthew 19:26

LIVE YOUR TODAY!

There is a hope for your eternity. And there is a hope for your today. God does not plan for your eternal salvation while neglecting your here and now. The redemptive life He offers is for today. So live your today!

Live the today God has always planned for you. Walk out the promises He has spoken into your life. No need to wait. No need to long after the day when the world is made new. Your life can be made new starting now.

The Scripture God inspired reminds you of the process. It is as if God is saying, "Yes. I knew the process of renewal would be difficult. That is why I am here. Trust Me."

Trust Him. And live your today!

. . .

For this very reason, make every effort to add to your faith goodness; and to goodness, knowledge; and to knowledge, self-control; and to self-control, perseverance; and to perseverance, godliness.

2 Peter 1:5-6

AND BE SEPARATE

The inevitable separation that comes between the believer and unbeliever is a separation that happens on its own. It happens for the simple reason that you choose differently because you are a believer who seeks Christ. It is not about making some public stand or moral point. When noticed, in fact, it may be quite uncomfortable. No one cheers you on for choosing different than they choose. But you cannot help, at some point, to choose differently.

And when you do begin to choose different in one matter or another, you may be uncomfortable, but you may also know that you are taking important steps in discipleship. You are moving beyond a mere belief in God to a place of truly following after Christ.

. . .

"Therefore come out from them and be separate," says the Lord. "Touch no unclean thing, and I will receive you."

2 Corinthians 6:17

THE LORD'S DISCIPLINE

When you approached God and asked for His help, when you asked for a life renewed, God was already there, waiting. Ready. But often God's process of renewal is not what you expect. You see and are concerned with your outer circumstances. God is concerned, first, with your heart.

God often disciplines via circumstances. Through your circumstances, in your response to them, you see how you are being renewed. You see how your thoughts affect your words and your words your actions. All are connected.

Difficult circumstances work in your favor when God is your teacher. Accept the new thought process He offers, and put these thoughts into action. In this way, God teaches you how to live.

God always works from the inside out.

. . .

"My son, do not make light of
the Lord's discipline, and do not
lose heart when He rebukes you."

Hebrews 12:5

WHO IS WISE?

Knowledge reaps pride, but wisdom reaps humility. Wisdom makes you to see beyond the self. It makes in you a teachable heart. A teachable life. And the teachable life is one able to experience all the blessings of what God can do. The teachable life is the life that learns to step when God says step and stop when God says stop. It is no longer concerned so much with outside appearances, no longer burdened with proving itself to itself or to others; because the wise, humble, teachable life knows the value of a life directed by God.

The life directed by God is the only life that carries eternal value. This is the life that lasts. The life worth living. The life renewed.

. . .

Who is wise and understanding among you? Let him show it by his good life, by deeds done in the humility that comes from wisdom.

James 3:13

A REVELATION

Both Scripture and time, all that is taking place in Creation, are part of the revelation of Christ, of who He is and why. And throughout Scripture you see, time and again, this revelation made to each individual heart, each individual life of those who know Him. Christ is known, first, as the Son of man, only to be revealed as Christ, the Son of God. Men follow Christ the man. But when they see Him glorified, when they see the risen Christ, the Savior, they fall at His feet. This is God!

Pray He reveals Himself to you as God. Pray your heart is open and listening. Pray you recognize Him and that you, too, fall immediately at His feet. Christ alone makes Himself known.

. . .

"When I saw Him, I fell at His feet as though dead. Then He placed His right hand on me and said: 'Do not be afraid. I am the First and the Last. I am the Living One.'"

Revelation 1:17-18

THE WORK OF YOUR HANDS

Have you prayed for God to establish the work of your hands? To bless and anoint the work He sets you to, whatever that work may be?

In your seeking God, in your family, in your relationship with others, in your career, whatever you do, let God be the One who establishes the work. The One to provide the work and set your hand to it. Acknowledge Him as the One who sets you in a place and sees you through.

When you acknowledge God as the Giver of all things, you acknowledge your own life in agreement with His. You acknowledge that your life is part of a much greater whole, a context that belongs first to God, your Father, who loves you.

. . .

May the favor of the Lord our God rest upon us; establish the work of our hands for us — yes, establish the work of our hands.

Psalm 90:17

NOT ALONE

You are not alone. You may feel alone. You may feel forgotten. Even so, God is with you. He has not failed you, nor will He fail.

God is near. He is here. And He has plans for your life, because your life is precious and pleasing to Him. Your prayer, sweet incense offered to your Father, the Great I Am.

The Maker of heaven and earth is pleased to call you His own. Even when you stumble, you do not fall, because He is with you. Always.

You are not alone. And your Father, who loves you, delights in your company, in your voice, in the sound of your laughter. So lift your head and rejoice! There is always hope, because there is always God.

. . .

The LORD is near to all who call on Him,
to all who call on Him in truth.

Psalm 145:18

THE ONLY LIGHT

Allow your heart, your mind, and every action of your day to draw you ever nearer
to Christ. You know how. The nearer to
Christ you live, the nearer to Him you
learn to abide, the more His light illuminates. The light of Christ reveals
every truth. And when you see truth, you
gain life. You can walk in life's true
context rather than the shadow of darkness.

In the shadow, you may come to believe
and live all number of false ideas. But
when you live near Christ, you see all
of Creation as it truly exists. You see
Creation within the context of God's
story, within the context of Christ and
His purpose.

Christ is the light. He is the only
light.

. . .

"When Jesus spoke again to the
people, He said, 'I am the light
of the world. Whoever follows Me
will never walk in darkness, but
will have the light of life.'"

John 8:12

TIMES TO REFINE YOU

The Lord allowed Joseph to go to prison for a crime he did not commit. Outward, it may have seemed God failed Joseph. It may have seemed that Joseph was obedient and God did not come through. But God saw beyond the present circumstance. Who knows but that Joseph needed this time with God, time of refining and testing? Joseph would one day have charge of all Egypt.

Difficult times, when yielded to God, refine you. God uses these times to mold your personality and character. These are the moments that make you who you are. The difficult moments made Joseph.

Joseph obeyed God and sought to honor Him, and even in prison the Lord was with him. God gave Joseph favor and blessed him.

· · ·

The LORD was with him; He showed him kindness and granted him favor in the eyes of the prison warden.

Genesis 39:21

A PRAYING LIFE

Your prayers are heard! Every one.
And they are collected by your Savior,
stored up by Him and received, held precious and close.

So pray often! Make your prayers, accepted as offerings, overflow. Christ
has washed away every sin, but the words
you say to Him He holds forever. Long
after you have forgotten the prayer, the
praise, the plea, your Jesus remembers.

It pleases Him to remember, and one day
you will see how He has kept every word.
He created you with His own hand and gave
His life to keep you. Do you know how
He rejoices over you? Do you know how
He treasures your words, your thoughts?
Not because He needs you. Because He
wants you.

. . .

When He had taken it, the four
living creatures and the twenty-four
elders fell down before the Lamb.
Each one had a harp and they were
holding golden bowls full of incense,
which are the prayers of the saints.

Revelation 5:8

Pray continually.

1 Thessalonians 5:17

"For I am the LORD,
your God, who takes
hold of your right hand
and says to you,
'Do not fear;
I will help you.'"

Isaiah 41:13

november

RIGHTEOUS LIVING

By Christ you are made righteous. By Christ you fulfill every command. Where the law fails, Christ succeeds. He replaces condemnation and failure with restoration and life eternal. Such is the glory of the Messiah that you are made new, into the person you were always intended to be.

To know Christ is to know yourself. To obey God in true righteousness is to obey by Christ. He is the One who enables you. He is the One who makes obedience possible. And so you no longer seek ways out of obedience. Rather, you seek a better obedience. You seek and press in to an obedience that comes from Christ, because His obedience is cleansing. His obedience reveals the truth of your life made whole.

. . .

Since they did not know the righteousness that comes from God and sought to establish their own, they did not submit to God's righteousness. Christ is the end of the law so that there may be righteousness for everyone who believes.

Romans 10:3-4

DWELL IN THE LIGHT

Plant yourself so near to God that you live and rest in His shadow. The shadow of the Almighty. Make yourself a resident in His presence. And when the enemy strikes, you can look quickly to God, because you are already there.

Call on the name of your God, and Christ Himself fights for you. His angels tend you. He still has a plan for you, and He is making the way. He clears your mind, your thoughts. He makes your eyes to see clear.

It is easy to become confused and disoriented in the day to day. The enemy is real and he enters through the weak places. But the longer you look on Christ and know His strength, the more secure life becomes.

. . .

He who dwells in the shelter
of the Most High will rest in
the shadow of the Almighty.

Psalm 91:1

ONE GOD

There is one God who loves you most, who takes you by the hand in pure self-lessness, and for the very reason that you are His and He is yours. He gives and does not take. He fills your life with His perfect purpose.

You praise Him because His name is great, and all the while He is reaching you. Pursuing you. There is only One called Love. One God who stills your fears and overcomes all on your behalf.

He helps you. He knows you. He fills the place in your life meant for Himself, because He knew nothing created could ever take the place of God, of the love He has for you.

God's love is for you and for always!

. . .

"For I am the LORD, your God, who takes hold of your right hand and says to you, 'Do not fear; I will help you.'"

Isaiah 41:13

THE GREAT VINE

One day you will look back and know yours was a life that experienced God. A true experience made real by the Vine. You will see the fruit of a life known by Christ. You will see the glorious way in which He works all things into good. Into right.

Until that day, trust the process. Trust that Christ is near, that He hears, that He prays for you. Savior of the world, acknowledge Him as a regular presence in your day. His presence is life. Is hope. Is rest and restoration.

Every day He guides you. He makes your steps worthwhile. And He loves you, not because of what you do – the fruit of your life is His – but because you are you.

. . .

"I am the vine; you are the branches.
If a man remains in Me and I in him,
he will bear much fruit;
apart from Me you can do nothing."

John 15:5

IF YOU LOVE ME

You know Scripture as a means of knowing Christ, and as a means of knowing His instruction. And if you obey Him, Jesus says, then you love Him. And if you love Him, you obey Him.

The call to obedience is direct and simple. A simple call for simple obedience. There is no other in the world you may follow as willingly and blindly as Jesus. What a relief to have One on whom you can rely so completely! What a wonderful, trustworthy Savior!

Obey Christ simply. As simply as possible. And when obedience becomes complicated, search your own heart. Ask whether the task is truly a complicated one, or are you merely trying to talk yourself out of God's will and into your own?

. . .

"If you love Me, you
will obey what I command."

John 14:15

ALL AUTHORITY, ALL GLORY!

Christ is all, enough, and more than enough! All authority rests with Him. All glory is His glory!

Often, you find yourself seeking a balance between humility and pride, selflessness and praise, giving and reward. But in the quiet, you realize no such balance exists. Christ is all and all is subject to Him. There is no room for pride, for selfish ambitions, for glory of the self, because all glory rightly belongs to Christ.

All attentions necessarily turn to Him. And when they do, all of creation is glorified because the One true Glory is in His rightful place! All of creation is glorified because when God is God, all else falls into perfect sequence. The broken become unbroken. All wrong is made right.

. . .

"Then Jesus came to them and said,
'All authority in heaven and on
earth has been given to Me.'"

Matthew 28:18

A STORY WITH THE FATHER

What do you ask of God, except you desire a place in His family? A story with the Father all your own? Somehow, though, jealousy creeps in at the thought of another's story. But history, Scripture, is full of individual stories that make up the collective family of God. Each one as unique as the next. Such is the glory and graciousness and creativity of God!

Father, forgive us when we are jealous. Help us rush to praise You, instead! Thank You, Lord, for all of these wonderful unique tales. You are weaving us together. Even though we are separate, we are one and all part of the same family. We know jealousy stems from pride and selfish desire. Grant us more of You!

. . .

If you harbor bitter envy and selfish ambition in your hearts, do not boast about it or deny the truth. Such 'wisdom' does not come down from heaven but is earthly, unspiritual, of the devil.

James 3:14-15

THE MERCIFUL

The merciful. Those who have themselves known mercy. Those whose remorse, whose fear and deep regret, has been met with grace, find their hearts relieved and eager to show mercy to others. These are the ones who know from experience that mercy begets mercy.

The future is shaped, in large part, by whether or not mercy is shown. The future is shaped, because hearts are shaped. Mercy makes a way forward, a way for fewer regrets.

To show mercy is to know a deeper understanding of Christ and His purpose. A person cannot know Christ and remain unwilling to know mercy. The two are inseparable.

Show mercy and you work toward a world where more mercy is shown, because more mercy has been known.

. . .

"Blessed are the merciful,
for they will be shown mercy."

Matthew 5:7

QUENCHING YOUR THIRST

When your mind is scattered, your heart heavy, when your day is confused, recognize that you need time alone with God. Sense and respond to the instinct in your heart toward the only One able to lift you, replenish you.

Your soul thirsts for God! Nothing takes the place of Him. He created you to need Him. And He allows you to know a void when He is not there. Praise God, He does not ask you to wait long before He escorts you to a place of worship! He allows you to know how missing Him feels, and then He ushers you into His presence.

Do not ask us to wait long, Lord. Our souls are thirsty. Do not ask us to wait long.

. . .

As the deer pants for streams of water, so my soul pants for You, O God. My soul thirsts for God, for the living God. When can I go and meet with God?

Psalm 42:1-2

WHAT IS GIVEN

John the Baptist knew his place. He had
a very clear understanding and acceptance
of the charge given him and did not want
any more or less than heaven's provision
and instruction. He wanted to fulfill the
life assignment given him by God, and to
do so meant operating within the life and
circumstances God provided.

Had John sought his own glorification, his
life would have pointed to himself rather
than to Christ and his purpose would not
have been fulfilled. But John had no
interest in taking the place of God. His
interest was Christ. Christ recognized.
Christ glorified.

John understood that no one takes the place
of Christ and no life is more worthwhile
than a life directed by Him.

. . .

To this John replied, "A man can receive
only what is given him from heaven."

John 3:27

STRENGTH THAT LASTS

You are strong! You are strong because
Christ is strong, and Christ is in you.
And the more of Him you know, and the
more of His truth you take as your own,
the more His strength manifests in your
life.

Strength of character, of awareness, of
steadfastness. Strength of knowing what
to say and when and how. Strength to
know Truth and to discern lies. Strength
for every occasion.

The strength that lasts, that overcomes,
is strength in Christ, and the only way
to know it is to know Christ and know
Him well. Christ defines strength and
He provides strength and He is strength.
Strength is a state of being with your
Lord. A state of understanding. A state
of leaning. Of trust.

. . .

Finally, be strong in the
Lord and in His mighty power.

Ephesians 6:10

EVERLASTING LOVE

In all your efforts to know God, to knock until the door is opened, you can rest assured that God is near. Calm your heart. Pray. Listen. No need to panic. You are not alone. The nearness of God depends on His faithfulness, not your own. And God's faithfulness is unending. He is near and ready to draw you.

The Spirit that overflows, the abundant joy, the calm and rest, all are available to you because of the glorious compassions and abilities of God. Though you have made mistakes, He has not abandoned you.

So still your heart. Wait patiently for Him. Steady yourself on the assurance that He is near and you are loved. You are loved with an everlasting, never-ending love.

. . .

"I have loved you with an
everlasting love; I have
drawn you with loving-kindness.
I will build you up again."

Jeremiah 31:3-4

WEAK WITHOUT HIM

Your life is a life of relationship. A life of experiencing God today to know Him more tomorrow. And of finding you know Him most of all in your weakness.

Weakness, limitation, reminds you that God is all. Weakness reveals grace and makes you to experience God's perfect ability and compassion. God did not create you to be independent or self-sufficient. He created you to be His. He created you to function at your very best when you have, in a sense, become your least. And when He has become your all.

God knows the best you is the you that loves and trusts Him. The you whose confidence in His ability is such that you scarcely take notice of your own limitations.

. . .

The Lord said to him, "Who gave man his mouth? Who makes him deaf or mute? Who gives him sight or makes him blind? Is it not I, the Lord? Now go; I will help you speak and will teach you what to say."

Exodus 4:11-12

A GREAT JOURNEY

God alone understands the full necessity of trial, of suffering. No one is spared. Christ Himself was not spared. He could have spared Himself. He is able to spare the trials of any one of His flock. But He doesn't. He allows you to experience refinement.

And so you accept the end result is worth every obstacle, and you run your race. You embrace each challenge, determined to triumph over fear and own every lesson offered.

Though the perseverance proves messy, difficult, overwhelming, you push through. Because the other side is a new place of understanding, a new vision of God, a new sense of His Spirit. And the journey is your call. The journey is where you meet Christ and the love of God.

. . .

The God of all grace, who called
you to His eternal glory in Christ,
after you have suffered a little while,
will Himself restore you and make
you strong, firm and steadfast.

1 Peter 5:10

PURE, BEAUTIFUL GOD

The purity of God is more wonderful
than the mind fathoms. The completeness
of His grace beyond understanding. But
the story continues to unfold and, one
day, you will know. One day everyone
will know! Hearts will comprehend and
questions will find answers.

Today you see confusion. God sees beginning and end and restoration! And
this God who is more than you realize,
realizes you completely. Accept the
miracle that is God at work and rejoice!
You are forever His and forever loved.

Though Creation does not now comprehend
Him, He makes Himself known. He makes
hearts to know Him and seek Him. And
in His perfect time, every heart will
be humbled. All will see His face. The
pure, beautiful face of God.

. . .

"For My thoughts are not your
thoughts, neither are your ways
My ways," declares the LORD.

Isaiah 55:8

PRAISE HIM!

Devote your heart to the Lord. Trust Him. He is full of mercy. Full of Truth. His grace overwhelms. Abounds. Lift up your soul in intimate worship, awestruck by the presence of the great I Am!

His devotion to you is unending. His pursuance undeterred, constant. When you are empty, He fills you. When you are weary, He gives rest.

No one is devoted to you as He. Praise His name, because He is perfect and His love knows no bounds. Because He is God, you praise Him. Because in Him you have found life and every good thing.

You praise Him because He is marvelous. You praise Him because He is near. He is the Creator, and He is with you, here, today.

. . .

I will praise You, O Lord my God, with all my heart; I will glorify Your name forever.

Psalm 86:12

THE MESSIAH IS COMING

Christ. The Messiah. He spoke to the Samaritan woman to say, "I am He." And He speaks to you. "I am the One you have waited for. The missing piece. Life fulfilled."

Jesus does not ask you to quench your own spiritual thirst. Rather, He came that He might quench it for you. He came that you might know Him and that, in knowing Him, you would find all that makes life complete.

All meaning, all purpose, is found in Him. And when you have Him, nothing takes Him from you. He is the One able to make you complete and the One prize you can never lose.

You cannot lose Christ, because Christ does not depend on you. You depend on Him.

. . .

"The woman said, 'I know that Messiah' (called Christ) 'is coming. When He comes, He will explain everything to us.' Then Jesus declared, 'I who speak to you am He.'"

John 4:25-26

REJOICE!

Live life to rejoice, always aware of God's love. You belong to the Creator of all things. Will you, then, be anxious? Will you allow your heart to fret, your mind to worry? Rather, remember that all things are in His hands.

Rejoice! Rejoice, because, truly, there is no fear for the one whose hope is in the Lord. He is making all things new and right. And you are invited to live today with tomorrow's renewal in mind. You are invited, reminded, to rejoice, because the life you live is not held by the worries of this world. Today's worries, whatever they may be, are temporary and non-binding. And so you rejoice!

You rejoice, because the promises of God are alive in you!

. . .

Rejoice in the Lord always.
I will say it again: Rejoice!
Philippians 4:4

ALIVE TO GOD

Alive to God. You! You are alive to God, because of the beautiful sacrifice of your Savior. Because of Christ, you are enabled to grant God His rightful place. To love Him with all your heart, mind, and soul. To choose others before yourself, because you choose God first.

This blessed gift of life renewed was not available to you in sin, because the nature of sin is to grant some other the place that belongs to God. But when you are dead to sin, you are dead to the idea that any may take His place.

So you choose God, because you choose life. And who better to teach you life than the giver of life Himself? The One who gives you breath? God?

. . .

In the same way, count yourselves dead to sin but alive to God in Christ Jesus.

Romans 6:11

DRAW NEAR

This God who loves you, who created you, He knows exactly who you are. He knows who He created you to be. He knows you far more than you know yourself.

Draw near to Him! The more you know of God, the more you know of you. The more you seek Him, the more you listen, the more you acknowledge Him and allow God to be God, the more you become the you He always intended for you to be.

God has a way of making His children come alive! He has a way of planting them in circumstances that refine and reveal the greatest potentials. He is never limited in His understanding, in His resources, in His vision for your future. So draw near!

. . .

In all your ways acknowledge Him,
and He will make your paths straight.

Proverbs 3:6

POINT OF VIEW

Your Jesus, your Savior who meets you in the present place, He grants a new point of view. He carries your attentions from the seen to the unseen. He makes you to know the eternal Truths, the eternal realities.

And Jesus is more than every motive. He is the presence, the strength, the wisdom that moves you. Lord, Spirit of God, He moves you! He is the point of view from which you know life. The point by which you view all.

From this mindset you discover a new self with new thoughts, ideas, and priorities. You view, you understand, with a whole new set of eyes. Spiritual eyes. A perspective redeveloped. A new point of view granted by the true, the living, God.

. . .

So we fix our eyes not on what is
seen, but on what is unseen.
For what is seen is temporary,
but what is unseen is eternal.

2 Corinthians 4:18

GRACIOUS, RIGHTEOUS GOD

God knows compassion because He is compassion. He knows righteousness because He is righteousness. And in all His actions toward you, He does not act from emotion, but from being.

Forever. Permanent. Unchanging. I Am.

And this God who encompasses all that is graciousness, all that is goodness, love, is the same God who hears you. He turns His face to you. He listens. He reaches you. He meets you where you are that His existence may be glorified in your existence, in your life. Every day God is making you a testament to His love.

You are more than someone God sees. You are His created. His daughter. His beloved. His affection for you is not fleeting. Gracious, righteous God, He is for you!

. . .

The LORD is gracious and righteous;
our God is full of compassion.

Psalm 116:5

GOD WANTS YOU

You are the one God wants. You are the one Christ came to redeem. He did not offer His life for the mere words of your mouth, nor for your works. He did not suffer for the sacrifices you make. God wants you!

He wants you in His presence, in His space. He wants your adoration. He wants you to know Him as great, marvelous, never-lacking God!

Sit at His feet. Seek His face. Wait for Him. Worship! Acknowledge today this mighty God who loves your heart and waits to fill your soul. He wants you and created you to need Him more than you need any other. He created you in such a way that only by Him do you know life fulfilled.

. . .

> Through Jesus, therefore, let us continually offer to God a sacrifice of praise – the fruit of lips that confess His name.
>
> Hebrews 13:15

FILLED WITH THE SPIRIT

The fullness of God is available to you,
to your life. But how can you know His
fullness until you have grasped the depth
of His love? God Himself is love. How,
then, will you know Him if you do not know
love?

Pray that you might grasp the love of God,
the enormity of His affection for you,
for His church. Seek Him as a child seeks
a father who is good and understanding.
There is a place for you in His house and
you may ask Him to reveal it.

You may ask Him to reveal His love, to
make it known to you. Because how will you
know the fullness of God until you have
known the fullness of His love?

. . .

I pray that you, being rooted and
established in love, may have power,
together with all the saints, to grasp how
wide and long and high and deep is the
love of Christ, and to know this love that
surpasses knowledge – that you may be filled
to the measure of all the fullness of God.

Ephesians 3:17-19

EVERYTHING FOR GOD

To give up everything you have is to give up everything in order to gain Christ. It is an acknowledgment that you are His and everything you once called your own is at His disposal. It is the realization that you are being made into the likeness of Christ, and to be made in His likeness is to grant yourself wholly to God.

The everything you give includes your thoughts, your opinions, your current understanding of the world. Though your circumstances do not change, though troubles remain, you meet them different than before. You live with a new response and, thus, gain new life.

You live different because you are different. Because you know that God is God and discipleship the way of heaven.

. . .

"In the same way, any of you who
does not give up everything
he has cannot be My disciple."

Luke 14:33

FROM EXPERIENCE

David was a man after God's own heart. He loved God. He sought Him. He worshiped God and danced before Him in praise. And he was a man who failed. David was a man of mistakes and set backs. He was a man who succeeded when he sought God and failed when he forgot Him.

When David spoke of God, of His goodness and the necessity of Him, David spoke from experience. He spoke as one who knew the promises of God to be true and knew the consequences of life without Him.

Speak from experience! Seek His face always. Seek the face of your God! Know His strength. And when you slip, when you fall, remember the Lord. Return. Return and praise His name.

· · ·

Look to the LORD and His strength;
seek His face always.

1 Chronicles 16:11

LIVE WITH ANTICIPATION

However long you have prayed, do not shy away when the opportunity for freedom, the answer, comes. Do not look, hope, pray and wait from pure habit or routine. Pray and expect! Anticipate. And when the wait ends, when the instructions come, praise God! He has heard and He calls you to action.

It would have been easy for the Israelites to dismiss Moses and the message he presented. The people had been oppressed for several hundred years. Why did God respond now? Why not sooner?

But they did believe Moses. They believed the message God sent to them. They worshiped. They accepted the answered prayer. God sees the full extent of His story. He knows just how it should unfold. So pray. Expect. Anticipate!

. . .

They believed. And when they heard
that the LORD was concerned about
them and had seen their misery,
they bowed down and worshiped.

Exodus 4:31

ENCOURAGE ONE ANOTHER

The deceitfulness of sin prompts you to dismiss the necessity of Christ. It dismisses doubt and unbelief as insignificant feelings. You open your arms to God's mercy, and sin slowly creeps in. It whispers to your heart, "You have got this. No need to seek God today." Sin whispers a lie and your heart hardens slowly over time.

Disbelief, doubt, take root, and how can any accept grace who disbelieve? Either God is God, or He is not. You know He is!

For this you have Jesus! For this you have the church. The fellowship of believers who lift up, encourage, speak Truth and faith and belief. Belief inspires an abandoned trust not inappropriate to the mercies of God, but quite complimentary to them.

. . .

Encourage one another daily, as long as it is called Today, so that none of you may be hardened by sin's deceitfulness.

Hebrews 3:13

WHERE HE DWELLS

God is with you! His presence surrounds you. His Spirit resides alongside your spirit. Because you are His, you have become the temple of God.

The temple of God! The place where He dwells. Lives. The life into which He speaks and moves and makes His home. And where God dwells, He works and He blesses. To bless you pleases Him. To make you whole reflects the glory of His love.

He walks into the room, into your life, and He makes you into the holy place of God, the place where His Spirit is known and manifested. A place where others experience the presence of God, because to come near to you is to come near to Him. His love. His grace.

. . .

We are the temple of the living God. As God has said: "I will live with them and walk among them, and I will be their God, and they will be My people."

2 Corinthians 6:16

UNFORGETTABLE

The experience of His voice. His presence.
This amazing grace that moves you when you
are lost, that directs your steps, though
you walk in darkness. Lift your hands,
your face, your voice. Lift your feet and
dance! Dance alongside unforgettable God!

Sing His praise. Acknowledge God as the
perfect love of your life and open the
way for His Word, unhindered, to breathe
over you. God makes life unforgettable!
God makes life real. He brings meaning and
purpose.

He makes you dance in darkness. He makes you
able to embrace every hardship as a means
to knowing His love, to knowing Him. To
experiencing Him. The relationship is two-
way. You speak to God and He speaks to you
with words of life. Words unforgettable.

. . .

Let them praise His name with dancing and
make music to Him with tambourine and harp.

Psalm 149:3

Look, the Lamb of God,
who takes away the
sin of the world!

John 1:29

december

THE LAMB

Look! See the Lamb of God. Call out to Him. He is the One who makes you know God. He is the One who brings spiritual understanding to your soul. Shout the words, hallelujah, God be praised! The Creator of all! Do not allow Him to go a day without hearing your praises. Without hearing your voice calling Him.

Ask Him to draw you near. Ask Him to reveal His love. And when He does, run to Him! Run to the Lamb. Only God can make you know the things of God. Only Christ can reveal His glory.

Call Christ and ask Him to call you. To enable you to see, to know. And do not hesitate to run to your Lord. The Lamb.

. . .

"The next day John saw Jesus coming toward him and said, 'Look, the Lamb of God, who takes away the sin of the world!'"

John 1:29

WALK OUT GRACE

The life you have in Christ is a gift.
Explore it! Experience it. Walk out the
grace you have received, the favor of your
Lord. You have grace available to you. It
is already yours. So walk it out.

Walk, live, choose in faith simply because
Christ says it is so. He says grace is
yours, and by grace you embrace a new
life. A life fitting for the child of God.

And by this grace, by this gift, your mind
is set on things above. Mind and heart
turn to Christ, and life follows suit.
What you know in thought is made real in
the day to day, because you walk out the
promises of God in faith. You experience
His promises made true!

. . .

Set your minds on things above,
not on earthly things.

Colossians 3:2

STOP, AND BE STILL

Stop. Just stop. Listen. Listen for the voice of the Lord your God. Invite His presence to fill your soul. To fill your home. Your day. Your thoughts. Invite God in to all your coming and all your going. And for now, for this moment, stop.

Allow God to reset your thoughts, to refocus your mind. Every day you are pulled from Him. You are pulled by one circumstance or another. All day the noise vies for your attentions.

Stop and remember, God is God. Before all, God is God. Beginning and end, God is God. Above every circumstance. Above every cause. Every dilemma. First, always first, God is God.

Set your mind, your heart, to Him alone. Remember to stop. Remember to listen.

. . .

The LORD came and stood there, calling as at the other times, "Samuel! Samuel!" Then Samuel said, "Speak, for Your servant is listening."

1 Samuel 3:10

GOD'S WORD

Consider the Gospel. Meditate on God's Word. Allow Scripture time to work over your life, over your mind. Resist the urge to organize God into a few direct points. Rather, turn His story over in your heart. Absorb it. The words expand and search your soul when your mind is allowed to explore the vastness that is God and is Scripture.

Scripture is a great key to knowing God and, thus, to knowing more about yourself. You come to understand your own life as you come to understand it within the context of Christ.

In Scripture you observe Jesus. You consider what He has done, His actions toward Himself and His actions toward humanity. You see the important things of Christ when you see Scripture.

. . .

Do not let this Book of the Law depart from your mouth; meditate on it day and night, so that you may be careful to do everything written in it. Then you will be prosperous and successful.

Joshua 1:8

COME WITH ME

Christ came that He might speak to your heart. He came because of His great love for us.

This Lord of your life is the love of your life. There is no one like Christ. Christ is love. We love because He loves us.

Love Himself speaks into your life. Love offers to show you love. Christ wants to lavish His love, Himself, on you. Indeed, He already has. He stands in the gap for you. He prays for you. He fights for you. He rests with you in His arms.

He calls you to Himself. He invites you into His world. Into His love.

. . .

God is love. This is how God showed His love among us: He sent His one and only Son into the world that we might live through Him. This is love: not that we loved God, but that He loved us.

1 John 4:8-9

GOD IS GREAT

Jesus was able to come as the least for the very fact of His being the greatest. Only the greatest, the Messiah, could hold the position of least. He came to serve where no other could take His place.

Just as He came to teach and enable His children to die and live, He teaches and enables them to be least. Christ teaches service, community, caregiving. He teaches the importance of living beyond the self.

Jesus turns the norms of society, because society has been turned on its head. He came to show the better way. The best way. He came to illustrate how all of humanity benefits, becomes greatest, when all of humanity – when individuals – becomes least.

Least sets free the potential of Great.

. . .

"For who is greater, the one who is at the table or the one who serves? Is it not the one who is at the table? But I am among you as one who serves."

Luke 22:27

DEFINED BY GOD

In God, you find the definition of you.
He alone defines you. He alone knows the
complete you. Yet everyday others try
to define you. They tell you what you
are and tell you what you are not.

And so Christ came. He came because someone, something, other than Himself was
trying to define His people. His love.
He came to make clear the definition of
you by making clear the definition of
Himself.

You belong to God and He is the only One
with the right and ability to name you,
to define you. He is the only One who
has claim on your heart.

He came because He had claim. Because He
made you. Because He loves you like no
other is able.

. . .

So God created man in His own image,
in the image of God He created Him;
male and female He created them.

Genesis 1:27

THE WAY FORWARD

Christ came to give a way forward. He came as the way forward. Not as a suggestion. Not as an option, one among many, to choose, but as the single way. The single option.

This is fitting to the Son of God. As Lord, Christ is the only One capable of being life, of being the way. It is a position for Christ alone to hold and fill. A position for the One who loves you best.

You were never meant to carry the burden of life, never meant to define life. You were meant to know life by Christ. To experience life, experience the true nature of living, by experiencing the true nature of Jesus.

In Christ you know life, and you live forward.

. . .

For if, by the trespass of the one man,
death reigned through that one man,
how much more will those who receive
God's abundant provision of grace and
of the gift of righteousness reign in
life through the one Man, Jesus Christ.

Romans 5:17

BE SMALL

Be small. Be less. Do the menial task. Take time for others. Listen. Assist. Resist the urge to think of yourself as higher than you ought, because you long for God to be in His rightful place.

Do the small thing and you allow God to be big. You open yourself to the world-altering hand of the Lord, when you are willing to be less. Thy will be done.

The tiny details of life – honesty, integrity, gentleness, generosity – they make up the foundation of the Body of Christ. Christ centeredness in the seeming small details of character is the Christ centeredness that makes the Body of Christ useful in the world.

Small makes the difference. Small allows Christ to shine and reach and touch.

. . .

> He guides the humble in what is
> right and teaches them His way.
>
> Psalm 25:9

THE COST

Many are eager to follow Christ until the following costs. And the following will cost.

The cost is inconsequential when considered from the feet of your risen Jesus. Even so, today, the cost is felt. Is known.

But how would you know you had chosen Him without the pang of the cost? Others may say, "Look how she loves Jesus!" while your own conscience wonders, "Do I? What proof do I have?"

But when you choose Him at a cost, then you know you choose Him and Him alone. When you are humiliated, laughed at, when they say, "What a fool! She thinks she follows Christ," when friends leave and still you crave Him, then you know. When your heart pays the price, you know.

. . .

"Blessed are those who are persecuted
because of righteousness, for theirs
is the kingdom of heaven."

Matthew 5:10

CHRIST IS LIFE

Because Christ, who is your safe place, is life, you are free to embrace and experience every challenge life presents. And life is a challenge! But you do not fear, because life, its every struggle, work, and even its rest, is gifted you in Christ.

You live by Christ. You choose by Christ. By Christ, you are not overcome. By Christ you do not stand idly by while life happens around you or to you. Rather, by Christ you have life. You know life. You are part of life and life is part of you. Because life is Christ and Christ is life.

You long to embrace life, to partake of it; therefore, you embrace Christ. You know you cannot have one without the other.

. . .

"Jesus answered, 'I am the way and the truth and the life.'"

John 14:6

DIRECTED STEPS

God never asks you to understand or comprehend His plan. He asks you to trust Him. He insists that if you will know the full effect of the God-centered life, the full effect of Christ as Lord, then you must trust Him. And you must follow. You must understand your life is not your own.

You follow Him not because you seek some adventure, not because you look for praise or a pat on the back. You follow Him because you know that He is God. You follow Him because He knows the way. He is the way.

And when His leading seems uncertain, you follow all the more. You obey anyway, unwilling to miss God. Unwilling to miss what He has in store.

. . .

A man's steps are directed by the LORD.
How then can anyone understand his own way?

Proverbs 20:24

YOUR WORD, O LORD

You long to know God; therefore, know His Word. In His Word you learn of Him. In His Word you see Him. You hear Him. You discover the way He moves and works among men.

God gave the Scriptures that you might know Him more. That you might learn to recognize His hand at work, that you might discern His will.

The will of God is good and pleasing. It builds up. It cleanses. It breathes life. And the will of God is known in the Word of God. Determine your heart will know it well. Determine you will never be led astray because of a lack of knowledge, because of a lack of effort to know God's Word. To know God.

. . .

Your word is a lamp to my feet
and a light for my path.
Psalm 119:105

MARVEL AT HIS MAJESTY

Brilliant. Genius. Perfect. God. Consider the enormity of the Father! The complexity of the Trinity. No need to find neat solutions to every aspect of God. Rather, take the time to consider the vastness of Him. No need to explain God today. You will know Him more when you are able to rest in knowing less, when you are able to admit that God's thoughts are not your own and grasping the Creator of all the world is more than your mind can conceive.

Take the time to meditate on the presence of God, to consider His Word, to marvel at Creation. The God experience has many aspects, and each personality is a type created by God, each uniquely suited to bask in His glory.

. . .

Let the light of Your
face shine upon us, O LORD.

Psalm 4:6

THE COST OF REPENTANCE

There is a cost for repentance because repentance embraces a new way. The repentant heart admits the truth about sin, the truth about itself, and embraces the cost of the about-face. It chooses God's way and pays a temporal price for the turnabout.

Repentance is not about punishment. It is about owning up, taking responsibility, and accepting God's grace, accepting that, in fact, He paid the ultimate price. "Let us fall into the hands of the Lord," David said, "For His mercy is great; but do not let me fall into the hands of men."

Christ paid what you could not. The price you pay is in doing the necessary work to correct what you can.

His mercy is great, His understanding beyond measure!

. . .

But the king replied to Araunah, "No, I insist on paying you for it. I will not sacrifice to the LORD my God burnt offerings that cost me nothing."

2 Samuel 24:24

WHO KNOWS?

Is it your place to choose how you will serve or to what extent you will obey? No. It is God's place, of course. He is the One who knows all. And so, you do not tell God what you will do. You do not wait for Him to make way for your own agenda, make way for your plans. Rather, you know God and you obey Him today. You seek His will, His way, for now.

You allow God to open the doors He sees fit and you do your best to walk in obedience as His leads. You do not know where He will take you. You do not know what circumstance will arise.

God alone knows the moments you were created for.

. . .

Who knows but that you have
come ... for such a time as this?
Esther 4:14

DRAW NEAR

Jehovah, He is your God. Your Father.
Ask Him to help you know His presence.
Ask Him to help you recognize His voice,
to know His Spirit, to understand His
Word, the necessity of Him.

God alone makes Himself known. He turns
your heart to His, to worship. He teaches you how to seek Him and how to find
Him. Ask Him to turn your heart.

Ask your Father God to grant you a teach-
able nature, a nature that embraces His
Truth, unwilling to remain as you are.
Unwilling to remain untouched by the
Creator.

He sees you and He loves you. He knows
you. He knows you better than you know
yourself. Will you, then, hide from Him?
Will you resist in any area?

. . .

Let us draw near to God with a sincere
heart in full assurance of faith,
having our hearts sprinkled to cleanse
us from a guilty conscience and having
our bodies washed with pure water.

Hebrews 10:22

THE PLAN IS GOD'S

You know the One who knows, and that is enough. When you follow God, when you trust Him, when you obey, you experience God's plan. You take your place in His story.

No need to fret over God's will for you. No need to uncover and define what He has in store. Simply trust Him. Know Him. He is enough.

God does have a plan. The mistake is when you believe you must gain prior knowledge. The mistake is when you seek the plan and its culmination more than you seek God.

The plan, insofar as you are concerned, is an afterthought. God is first. He must be first. You are His. The plan also is His. Only He brings your life to appropriate fruition.

. . .

Is anything too hard for the LORD?
Genesis 18:14

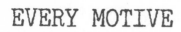

EVERY MOTIVE

God will not be fooled. You may be able to fool others. You may fool yourself. But God knows the heart. He understands every motive. When you speak a word, your every action, God sees the root of it.

He sees what moves you. He knows where your devotions lie, whether with Himself, with yourself, or with some other. He knows, even when you do not, whether you are self-serving or God-serving.

And so you turn your ear and heart to God, because He makes you know too. He allows you to know the depth of your depravity that you might know the necessity of Christ.

God knows your motives and He is able to purify. He is able and He is willing.

. . .

The LORD searches every
heart and understands every
motive behind the thoughts.

1 Chronicles 28:9

SLOW TO ANGER

Anger has a way of taking control of a person's life and dominating every area. No part of your life remains untouched once anger is given rein. It is a difficult emotion to conquer, especially when anger has been years unchecked. But ignore anger and anger will take you over, because anger will certainly not ignore you.

Anger keeps you from God, keeps you from His healing grace. To be slow to speak and quick to listen, eager to embrace humility before Christ is no easy pursuance. For most, to embrace humility and put away anger takes a consistent going before God, a daily accepting of and putting on of His grace. A daily reminding of the self that only God is God.

. . .

Be quick to listen, slow to
speak and slow to become angry,
for man's anger does not bring about
the righteous life that God desires.

James 1:19-20

TO KNOW GOD

God's will for your life – your purpose – is to know God. Nothing in life comes to proper fruition until you begin to know Him, until you know Love and how you are loved. How much you are loved.

The perfect love of God brings all else into perspective. It both challenges and brings you rest. It inspires and comforts. It explains what you would not other-wise understand.

And when you desire, honestly, to know God, to know His love, to hear Him, He makes Himself known. He helps you see. He helps you know Him.

God is a mystery, but He is a mystery who explains Himself. He does not stay hidden from your heart's eye. He grants Himself to you for love. For life.

. . .

"Now this is eternal life: that they may know You, the only true God, and Jesus Christ, whom You have sent."

John 17:3

FOLLOW HIS EXAMPLE

The Messiah was coming. And one day He would say to His disciples, "Do as I have done. Follow My example." He would say to His followers, "Accept humiliation that others might see Me."

The Messiah would present a radically different, radically new way, and He would say, "Follow My lead." He would defeat death and, then, He would ask you to die. Die to your way and embrace His own. Die to your agenda and accept that His is better. Accept, trust, that when you embrace the Life, the Truth, of Christ, you embrace an existence far more real than any existence without Him.

And when you lay down your own life, you make way for others to see and embrace Him too.

. . .

"I have set you an example that you should do as I have done for you."
John 13:15

EVERLASTING GOD

Christ alone brings Creation full cir-
cle. You could not exist without Him. He
makes you exist. In the same way, Christ
knew you could not rightly die unless He
took your death on Himself. You neither
live nor die without the life of Christ.

And so He came. He came because Creation
was not yet complete. Today, it is not
yet complete. He comes again.

Christ came to teach how to die and to die
for you, and to teach you how to live.
He is life that you may know life. He is
goodness, that you may know goodness.
He is love, that you may know love.

Everlasting to everlasting, He is God!
Creator who continues to create, to make
you complete, even today.

. . .

Before the mountains were born
or You brought forth the earth
and the world, from everlasting
to everlasting You are God.

Psalm 90:2

december 24

SON OF GOD

Though it seemed impossible, He came.
Christ. The Messiah. God with us. Immanuel.
He came because nothing is impossible with
Him; and He came because, without Him,
nothing is possible.

With Christ all is made complete. His
coming was essential to God's story, essential to Creation. The very necessary
part of the process. And today the process
continues.

The story did not happen and end. Rather,
the Magi saw the star. They looked forward
to Christ, and you look back to when He
came and forward to when He will come
again. His birth was a step in the making
of your own spiritual birth, of your own
life, of the lives of those around you.

He came as Life. To make all things possible.

. . .

"The angel answered, 'The Holy Spirit will
come upon you, and the power of the Most
High will overshadow you. So the holy one
to be born will be called the Son of God.
For nothing is impossible with God.'"

Luke 1:35, 37

THE SAVIOR IS BORN

Today you celebrate that Christ is born!
You celebrate that He is Lord, that He
is near, that He gave you His very life.

He is the One who loves you most. He
could have created you and given you
no idea of His existence. Instead, He
created you and then He came and lived
with His created. He came and felt what
you feel. He heard what you hear. He
experienced what you experience.

He took the necessary steps to insure
you would not merely hear stories about
Him, but you would hear about Him from
Him.

Perfect God, Lord above all, who does
not place Himself out of reach, but becomes man that man, that you, might know
Him more.

Perfect Savior. Precious Lord!

. . .

"Today in the town of David a Savior has
been born to you; He is Christ the Lord.
This will be a sign to you:
You will find a Baby wrapped
in cloths and lying in a manger."

Luke 2:11-12

december 26

THE COURSE

From Bethlehem to Egypt to Nazareth. This was the course. Who could have known? The path of the Savior took years to fulfill. The details of prophecy come together over time and in unexpected, often mundane, ways.

How important to trust God and follow His course! His directives do not always make sense to you, but eventually the trails of obedience, the trusting, the following begin to intersect.

The most satisfying moments are the ones that have been clearly orchestrated by God in hindsight. These are the moments when you followed blindly. You trusted, because God is the One you trust. The path did not seem to make sense.

But then, a revelation! This is God. He follows His own course and invites you along.

. . .

"He went and lived in a town called Nazareth. So was fulfilled what was said through the prophets: 'He will be called a Nazarene.'"

Matthew 2:23

TELL HIM

Your God is majestic. Tell Him! Acknowledge the perfect dignity of God to God. Acknowledge to Him the impressive work of His hands. Tell Him that you see, that you notice the creation He has made, that you want to hear His voice, to know His Word.

Acknowledge the immanence of God and remind yourself of your own tiny place before Him. Of your own dependent position as the created. As the one who relies on God for life, for breath.

The glory of God is set above the heavens. No one can take the place of your God. No other can do what He has done. And so you tell Him. You acknowledge. You recognize His position, His authority, as the only Almighty God.

. . .

O LORD, our Lord, how majestic is
Your name in all the earth! You have
set Your glory above the heavens.

Psalm 8:1

LIFE REVEALED

The death of Jesus. Salvation of the world. Salvation for you. Salvation, because the One who is Judge judged Himself. The One who is everything became nothing for the sake of His church. He did what you could not do. He took the judgment you could not bear.

And now, you carry His death in your body, in your life. You forfeit your rights, your opinions, yourself, that others might see Him. Might see Christ. What is temporal loss when compared to Christ and eternity? You lose your life in the hope that others may gain, because Christ Himself lost His life for you, and for the others.

Heaven forbid the saints should stand in the way of the lost, in the way of the cross.

. . .

We always carry around in our body the death of Jesus, so that the life of Jesus may also be revealed in our body.

2 Corinthians 4:10

NOW YOU ARE LIGHT

Now you are light. You are steadfast. You are coming to know the Word of God, and the Word of God makes you stable in an unstable world. The presence of God fills you with hope and joy.

You are light and no longer darkness, now that you have Christ. And your life is necessarily different because of Him. By His presence, your life grants an honest – though often distorted – glimpse of spiritual reality. Spiritual Truth. Or, at least, it should. It must. And it will when you follow Christ and allow yourself to be set into the motion of a life lived with God.

And by this light that is His light, others will see Him and come to know Him and trust Him.

· · ·

For you were once darkness,
but now you are light in the Lord.
Live as children of light.

Ephesians 5:8

EAGERLY AWAIT

The story is not over. Not your story.
Not God's. Christ came to the earth, the
earth He created, as Redeemer. He came to
fulfill every prophecy. He came to carry
your past and make way for your future.

Your life, your eternity, is in process.
And so you rejoice and embrace every
life challenge. You rest because Christ
came and you press on because Christ is
coming. You press on because the story is
in process.

And you are part of the collective story.
You are meant for every promise God made
to His children, His family. He chose you.
He came for you. He took every sin upon
Himself. He paid every debt, every price,
so that today you are His.

Eagerly await!

. . .

But our citizenship is in heaven.
And we eagerly await a Savior from there,
the Lord Jesus Christ.

Philippians 3:20

CHRIST'S APPEARANCE

Christ appeared once on the earth, and He will appear again. And when Christ appears, you will appear. Everything you are not will fall away and you will hear His voice saying, "This is who you are."

For the first time, you will fully recognize yourself, and you will recognize His voice. The voice of the Spirit of God. The same voice that directs you today, that leads you. You are never alone, and when Christ appears, He will be no stranger to your heart.

And you will be no stranger to His. Jesus Christ will look at your scars, and you will look at His. And both of you will know. Everything will be right and perfect, when next Christ appears.

. . .

When Christ, who is your life, appears, then you also will appear with Him in glory.

Colossians 3:4